BEHIND CLOSED DOORS

THE BABY BROKERS

By Belinda Conniss

BEHIND CLOSED DOORS

Copyright © 2020 by Belinda Conniss

No part of this book can be reproduced in any form or by written, electronic or mechanical, including photocopying, recording, or by any information retrieval system without the written permission in writing by the author.

Although every precaution has been taken in the preparation of this book, the author/publisher assume no responsibility for errors or omissions. Neither is any liability assumed for damages resulting from the use of information contained herein.

ISBN: 9781727213317

Printed in by
Amazon

Acknowledgements

I would like to acknowledge everyone who over the last four years have taken the time to welcome myself and husband Jerry in the first instance to Sean Ross Abbey, Roscrea Tipperary.

For trusting me in telling me a little of their story which we all can appreciate is not only heartbreaking but still very raw.

I would like to extend my thanks to Philomena Lee and her daughter Jane who were the first people I met on that first visit to SRA, who talked to me about Anthony Lee *(Michael Anthony Hess)* May he RIP. To Teresa Collins and Michael Donovan for keeping me up to speed and who have become very good friends to myself and Jerry.

And to all who attend the commemoration every year, those who I have spent time with including Susan Drew. Last but not least Mary Lowler, who sent me the link to read all about it, without that I wouldn't be aware of the situation. Jerry and I will always know you as, our "Irish Family" And as the saying goes.

'May our friendship be as long as the road to Tipperary'

We love you all.

Table of Contents

Foreword 1

Acknowledgements 3

Introduction 7

Scandal That Shook The Nation 9

Lost Children of Tuam 15

Tuam 19

Sean Ross Abbey 29

Commemorations 2017 50

Commemorations 2018 55

Commemorations 2019 60

Opening of the Big House 65

Teresa's Story 76

Mary's Story 108

Added News 145

Resources 150

INTRODUCTION

Most of us are aware of the scandal that has hit the headlines this last several years in regard to the mother and baby home and the magdalene laundries era.

This book has been written to further highlight the situation surrounding the reports we are hearing about.

The stories of some of the woman that you are about to read have been included to show our support for those born in such institutions and to their biological mothers.

We have to remember that for some of the woman who were placed in such institutions had a very different experience, some did not experience what many others did.

At the time of writing, I am led to believe the Republic of Ireland still do not allow adopted children full access their documentation regarding their adoptions.

I want you to know as you read this book why I have written it and what's on my mind, and for you to understand, that for the survivors, many of whom feel separated from the very existence one would expect from life, like many woman they have a story.

My own faith has now been misplaced by cracks, I have been tested, there was a time when I would faithfully go to mass to receive Holy Communion. I believed? This was the only way in which to show my maker my appreciation for the life he has given me.

I was wrong, I soon came to realise that I/We have a private and personal relationship with God.

One in which we do not and should not bow to any statue or follow any rules in as far as the church goes. This realisation, came to me upon first hearing of the atrocities of the church and state in Ireland and around the world.

Through research, which has now proven to me that to follow any church, I/We are actually following a cult, which we are sucked into through lies and deceit. What you are about to read are accounts of which took place in a very religious Ireland as told to me by some individuals who experienced it.

And It wasn't only the Catholic church that were involved in these situations it was other religions too. Some of the things you'll read may be a little disturbing but they are stories that shook the nation and must be told.

I along with many others did not think that the very faith we follow/followed were actually breaking their own rules, nor that many knew what was happening yet done nothing to stop it.

So where did it all begin, when did it end, has it ended?

SCANDAL THAT SHOOK THE NATION

As reported by, *The Journal Ireland*

The disclosure of child abuse, illegal adoptions of children in religiously affiliated institutions is more widespread than we first thought, and that is only the cases we know about.

Thousands of cases throughout such institutions like mother and baby homes, magdalene laundries and orphanages etc, which were run by the very people who are/were supposed to protect them, particularly those which were run by the Catholic, and Protestant churches and possibly many others.

There may have been as many as *15,000* or more? Forced illegal adoptions to have taken place in Ireland alone, right up until the late *1980s*, yet astonishingly for the vast majority, no files are readily available or seem to exist?

Now, here in the twenty-first century, we look back on that stigmatisation in which we can only imagine how bad those dark days must have been for those concerned.

According to the Journal Ireland that in the twentieth century mother and baby homes became increasingly common.

And from the *1920s* onwards, mother and baby homes or Magdalene laundries run by the Magdalene order were under religious jurisdiction.

A number of voluntary organisations, called for adoption to be legalised in the *1930s, 40s* to regulate the number of babies being sent abroad for adoption from the homes.

However, the majority of Europe had legalised adoptions by the end of the *1920s* (Including Britain). DeValera, Considered introducing 'Adoption Legislation' in *1938,* but was shot down on the basis, "The Religious problems would almost inevitably involve the government in difficulties".

Yet, a system called 'Boarding Out' facilitated an underhand system of adoption in, and from Ireland prior to *1952*.

A letter written by the Hollywood actress, *Jane Russell*, in *1951* to the 'Irish Times' in which she expressed her immediate desire to adopt. 'An Irish Child' shows that even prior to the legislation of adoption in Ireland, it was still possible.

In *1951* there were over *120* adoption passports accounting for *7.7%* 'Illegitimate' births in Ireland were issued.

Ultimately, the procedure for legalising adoption in Ireland was a long religious battle.

The now infamous, *Archbishop John C. McQuaid,* was consulted on the issue of legalising adoption in Ireland in *1945,* even before and at the end of the Second World War, the heads of the mother and baby homes were writing to the government to request more funding, the system was feeling the strain.

So why? Was it another seven years before adoption was legalised in Ireland? It was mainly due to objections from the Archbishop.

McQuaid, who was considered 'The bogey of Proselytism,' e,g that Catholic babies might be adopted by Protestant families.

The department of justice approached the Archbishop on the matter in *1948*.

After a few meeting, Minister for Justice *General MacEoin* discontinued the matter stating that; "The department had been unable to devise any provisions which would overcome Dr McQuaid's objections."

Neither McQuaid nor the government could ignore the issue of overcrowding in the mother and baby homes, nor the pressure put on the government by voluntary organisations such as, the Legal Adoption Society.

After the McQuaid's victory in the notorious mother and baby child scheme controversy, (In which Dr Noel Browne was forced to resign his post as Minister for Health for proposing healthcare that would provide sex education to young woman).

McQuaid was willing to negotiate an adoption bill, but on HIS terms, this took the form of the Episcopal Committee of legal adoption.

A committee of high ranking clerics who scrutinised every clause of the Adoption Act before it became law.

Even after they approved it there were more problems along the way, the Attorney General, firmly against the idea, stated that Ireland was a catholic country and while, 'This did not mean that parliament should be expected to penalise other creeds',

It meant that, other governments could not be asked to introduce legislation contrary to the teaching of. *'That Great Church'* Eventually, adoption legislation was approved with a number of clauses deemed essential by the Catholic clergy.

Introducing the clause meant that, children could only be adopted by people of the same faith.

The Adoption Act *1952* became law on first day of January *1953,* Overseas adoption continued even after the legalisation of adoption, the overriding concern for illegitimate children was their religion.

Deputy, *Maureen O'Carroll* received an extremely, hostile reaction in the Dail in *1956,* when she questioned the number of children under seven to be adopted abroad, but this did not apply to illegitimate children aged over one year, a key example of the attitude towards illegitimacy at the time.

Minister for External Affairs *Desmond O'Malley* assured the Dail in the aftermath of Deputy O'Carroll's concerns, 'that, *the requirements of my department concerning the issues of passports for the adoption of children are very stringent,'* he continued, *in all these cases appropriate religious organisations in the adopting countries investigate the cases concerned.* The matter was then dropped.

Reforms were made to the Act in the *1960s,* but it was until the *1970s* that it was overhauled and significantly, this time it was done without consulting religious authorities.

Calls for repeal of religious influence in adoption had come before that, such in the landmark case of J. McG and W. McG vs The Attorney General.

The ruling which allowed J. McG to adopt W. McG's son from a previous relationship despite not being the same religion as the child was a direct conflict to a clause which the Church had insisted so strongly in *1952.*

Attitudes to the Church's influence on education was clearly changing, and in *1972* was the first year since the *50s* in which no adoption passports were issued.

A stark difference from *1951* in which *122* were issued a key insight into the fact that Ireland's attitudes towards illegitimacy and overseas adoption was beginning to change.

The Reform Adoption Act, *1974* reflected these changing attitudes and crucially was drawn up with no influence from the Catholic church.

The Mother and Child Scheme controversy is often used as example of the influence clerical opinion has on the Irish governments of the mid twentieth century.

However, the subject of legal adoption and influencing the legislation, as well as, the evident fear of *'The Bogey of Proselytism'* is evident of the grip the Church had on both the government and society in Ireland.

THE LOST CHILDREN OF TUAM

Ireland Wanted to Forget, But the Dead Don't Always Stay Buried!

Written by Dan Barry in the New York Times Oct 28 2017

Behold a child.

A slight girl all of six, she leaves the modest family farm, where the father minds the livestock and the mother keeps a painful secret, and walks out to the main road, off she goes to primary school, off to the Sisters of Mercy.

Her auburn hair in ringlets, this child named Catherine is bound for Tuam, the ancient County of Galway town whose name derives from the latin for *"Burial Ground."* It is the seat of the Roman Catholic Archdiocese, a proud distinction announced by the sky scraping cathedral that for generations has loomed over factory and field.

Two miles into the long-ago Irish morning, the young girl passes through a gantlet of grey, formed by high walls along the Dublin Road that seems to thwart sunshine.

To her right runs Parkmore Racecourse, where hard-earned shillings are won and lost by the nose.

And to her left, the mother and baby home, with glass shards embedded atop its stony enclosure.

Behind the hidden divide, nuns keep watch over unmarried mothers and their children. Sinners and their illegitimate spawn, it is said; The fallen.

But young Catherine knows only that the children who live within seem to be a different species altogether, sallow, sickly and segregated. "Home Babies," they're called.

The girls long walk ends at the Mercy school, where tardiness might earn you a smarting whack on the hand. The children from the home are always late to school, by design it seems, to keep them from mingling with "Legitimate" students.

Their oversize hobnail boots beat a frantic rhythm as they hustle to they're likely slap at the schoolhouse door.

A sensitive child, familiar with the string of the playground taunts, Catherine nevertheless decides to repeat a prank she saw a classmate pull on one of these children.

She balls up an empty candy wrapper then, presents it to a home baby as if it still contains a sweet, then watches as the little girl's anticipation melts to sad confusion.

Everyone is laughing nearly, this moment will stay with Catherine forever.

After classes end, the home babies hurry back down the Dublin Road in two straight lines, boots tap-tap tapping, and disappear behind those Gothic walls.

Sometimes the dark wooden front door is ajar, and on her way home Catherine thrills at the chance of a stolen peek.

Beyond those glass-fanged walls lay seven acres of Irish suffering, buried here somewhere as the famine victims who succumbed to starvation and fever a century earlier when the home was a loathed workhouse for the homeless poor.

But they are not alone, deep in the distant future, Catherine will expose this property's appalling truths. She will prompt a national reckoning that will leave the people of Ireland asking themselves: *Who were we? Who are we?*

Source: www.nytimes.com/interactive/2017/10/28/world/europe/tuam-ireland-babies-children

TUAM

The story broke in the Irish Mail on Sunday, there was news of a mass grave in Tuam, Galway.

A former mother and baby home for unmarried mothers, of course, what caught my attention were the words *'Mass Grave'* Which is believed? To be the burial area of almost eight hundred children.

The home formally known as the old workhouse in *1918,* under the Irish Poor law was originally built in *1846* and housed around *800* people, the main building contained an infirmary and what they called an *'Idiots Ward'*

I had decided to look into the mother and baby home to find out more and began reading about Catherine Coreless the woman who had discovered this information.

The more I read, the more horrified I became, not only from what I have read but from hearing peoples stories and watching interviews conducted over this last couple years or so.

The home run by the Bon Secours Nuns, ran from *1925* until *1961* and catered for thousands of unmarried mothers and their illegitimate children.

According to reports as many as *796* children died of various illnesses, including TB, Pneumonia, Malnutrition, Convulsions and so much more.

I must be honest, the amount of children who died each year of those illnesses does bother me, are there questions to be asked here? *'I think so'.*

For example; In the year *1925* there were *thirty-six* deaths ranging in ages from four weeks old to eight years.

Of the *thirty-six, twenty-three* had measles, ranging from *nine* months old to eight years.

I did find this a little odd so, I decided to check if there was an outbreak of measles in Galway in *1925*? I had found nothing, however, that's not to say it wasn't true.

I found a public health report for Galway, whereby the dates stopped at *1911* and began again in *1926*? Although I also found this rather strange it's not to say that a report is non-existent.

Jumping to *1934* nine years later, they had *twenty-two* deaths ranging from *seventeen* days to a little over one year of varied illness, the lists go on and on.

We have to take into account, that these are just some of the figures I have found while doing my research, the mortality rate could be much lower and or higher through various years.

The home is now under investigation not only relating to the deaths of many children but also to find the relevant records assuming they can be found?

Excavations had been carried out between November *2016* and February *2017* and what was found was a significant amount human remains ranging from foetal to around three years which were interred in a vault with *twenty* chambers.

The commission of investigation were appalled by what they had found, They said; they would continue the investigation into who was responsible? For disregarding human remains in such a manner.

So, who was responsible For such atrocities? Some say the church? Others say the state, since doing my research I believe it is most definitely both.

The home had been taken over in *1925* by the Bon Secure sisters, led by Mother Hortense McNamara, by now a place for unwed mothers to be sent to give birth to their babies.

The mothers were required to live in the home for a period of one year after giving birth to their babies and work *(Unpaid)* for the nuns.

This was to pay back the nuns for services rendered.

According to research I've done and people I have spoken to, the woman were treated as slaves, a punishment they had to endure for being sinners.

The woman's children were kept separate from them so they couldn't bond with each other, not all woman of course were kept too far away from their children, but for many they hadn't even got to hold them after they were born.

In *1947* a report by an official inspector stated, he had visited the home and noted some of the children had been suffering from malnutrition, and some of the children examined were described as being emaciated and the homes were overcrowded.

The report also stated that in *1943 34%* of the children died in the home, in *1944 25%* in *1945 23%* and in *1946 27%.*

Although the figures are up and down these were still a large percentage of child deaths. *What I found hard to comprehend,*

The inspector stated,

'The care given to the infants in the home is good, the sisters are careful and attentive. <u>Diets are excellent</u>?'

I mean really? In one hand he is saying that the children are suffering from malnutrition, *yet*, he goes on to say their diets are excellent? He then went on to say; *'It is time to enquire the cause of deaths before they get much higher'?*

Remember, there were a vast number of children who died from malnutrition, there are so many discrepancies in the various research I have undertaken which makes it a little harder to write this book, but I have chosen to carry on with what I have been able to find and include some of these discrepancies.

It is thought that as many as *1000* or more children were sold to couples overseas, some noted to have been sold for as much as *$2000* which was a vast amount of money back then.

But what gave the church the right to take a child from their mother, sell that child to another family for monetary gain?

What makes it even worse, the state knew this was going on and did absolutely, *Nothing!* However, it doesn't really surprise me, because while doing my research I have come to discover that, 'What the church say pretty much goes'.

I don't just mean only the sale of children, then again who knows? It was all kept under wraps back then, who is to say things aren't still going on that shouldn't be? The church has hidden many a secret back then, most likely still do, their rules as far as what we can ask or even see is still forbidden.

Another article I read in the Tuam Herald, stated; *"Catherine Corless had uncovered a case whereby a mother had been found working in England while the nuns cared for her child in the home back in Ireland, the mother, had been sending payments for her child not knowing that the child had actually been fostered out and the nuns had been keeping the money"*

A lot of the children had been sent to the States to Clergy to be illegally adopted out, its also a known fact that the children's names had been changed as were their mothers this was so that there would be no trace or at least they hoped there would be no trace of that child finding out their true identity.

Whilst doing my own family tree, I discovered that many of the adopted who have done their DNA on Family Heritage sites, came to discover that their biological fathers were priests.

The sad reality of those dark times is simply, the church took advantage of many families, and their daughters, who for many reasons, some due to being sexually abused, became pregnant.

In the eyes of a very strict Catholic society, those woman were sinners they had to be punished, the church saw this as an opportunity, they stole, and robbed from their families.

There were also letters that were sent to the parents asking for money to keep their daughters children, including some that had already died and or been discharged.

Another report stated that, If thousands of babies/children were illegally adopted to the States, without the willing consent of their mother, then that practice would have been facilitated by doctors.

Social workers, religious orders and others who could possibly still be working within the system?

I know one thing for sure, even if they are no longer within the system, there will be some who may be elderly, and still alive to tell the story. Whilst many people in Galway say that this is no secret and that it was common knowledge, most refused to talk about it.

I heard one say in an interview aired on YouTube, that it was best left in the past, the attitude of many, I know that I and many others would disagree. I personally feel that although some of those involved are no longer around, the Vatican should take full responsibility for the actions of the past.

I do understand however, that it has nothing to do with our present Pope, but he could still do what is right to help those who suffered and continue to suffer.

The Vatican, must allow all documentation including birth certificates held to be released, this is not about redress its about human rights, its about knowing the truth, it's about the little one's who did not survive and were not given a proper burial.

Catherine Coreless, appeared on the Late, Late Show. Back in *2017* joining her were two individuals who have family buried at Tuam, including the journalist who broke the story.

Catherine received a standing ovation, the host Ryan Tubridy said; *"If the audience represents the people watching the show then there is a hunger for truth"*

I have to agree people need to know the truth no matter how dark and or horrendous that may be, not only do the church need to be held accountable, the survivors have the right to know what happened to their loved one's and where exactly they are buried.

The church and the state need to show that they stand with those who were so undoubtably wronged in those years.

Catherine was awarded the "Bar Council of Ireland's Human Rights Award" In the same year.

She was presented for 'Exceptional Humanitarian Services,' she responded with this short speech.

I couldn't get my mind around how the sisters could leave that home in 1961, close the gates when it closed down, with 796 children buried beneath in the tunnels in coffins.

A lot of them in the sewage tank area as we now know, what kind of mentality would leave that place without acknowledging that so many burials were there?

So many precious lives were lost, the ideal would be to exhume those little bodies, and just show them some dignity and reverence. Perhaps reinter them in the main Tuam graveyard, which is only across the road. Hopefully the commission of inquiry will give the survivors justice.

My work in campaigning on behalf of the survivors of the mother and baby homes continues. I hope that this special award will give even more survivors the strength to come forward to tell their story.

With each and every testimony, the truth is uncovered further and our campaign for justice to prevail is strengthened. I share this award with all survivors, this is for them.

In *1975,* two twelve year old boys were playing at the side of the mother and baby home, when, they found a hole/chamber under a concrete slab, they had found what was believed to be skeletal remains of children.

The concrete was thought to be the cover of the old septic tank from the home, whilst locals believed the remains to be that of the great famine, unbaptised and or stillborn babies.

The home closed its doors in *1961,* most of the occupants were sent to similar institutions, such as, (Sean Ross Abbey in Roscrea).

The building lay mostly disused until its demolition in *1972,* when a new housing estate was built on the site local residents recalled seeing nuns and workmen apparently burying remains in Tuam late in the night.

Back In *2010* the bodies of around *222* infants from Bethany house another maternity home, were found in a mass unmarked grave in Dublin.

After the news came out about Catherine Coreless findings which then led to the media.

(Before any fact-finding investigations took place)

And some commentators including locals preferring to believe the alternative, that the remains on the site were most likely to be bones of the famine era.

Bones of the famine victims were indeed found back in *2012* and archaeologists determined that they were of the *Nineteenth* century paupers from the Tuam poor law union workhouse.

A solicitor representing former residents said; *The number of recorded deaths at the Tuam home over thirty years was off the scale, Comparing that of the rate elsewhere at the same time, according to the records, there was a large archive found of photographs, documentation and correspondence, relating to children being sent for adoption to the States, so the proof is there!*

I can, and I'm sure the public can understand? The full scale of this situation, and why it's important that the church and state now do what is right. There has been far too much heartbreak in the past, yet, the heartbreak continues.

Is it so hard to hold their hands up and say, we are so sorry for past atrocities? Is it so hard to put their hand in their pocket and pay for these investigations to continue until there is some sort of resolution?

It seems that the church do not want nor will they allow the full scale of what happened be revealed, neither do they want the world to know that, they have taken money from those who bought the children they stole.

SEAN ROSS ABBEY

The first time I visited Sean Ross Abbey Roscrea, Tipperary was back in *2017*, I had previously been invited by a long time social media friend prior to *2017*, but due to travel commitments was unable to attend.

My friend Mary posted a link about a mother and baby home in Co Galway.

I messaged her to ask what it was all about so she tagged me in the post which I then went on to read.

It was about skeletal remains found in a septic tank in Tuam, I was horrified when I read the story.

I asked my husband to accompany me as it was my first time going to the commemorations, I had researched and read what I was able to find online about SRA before going so that I had a handle on what exactly took place at this event every year.

To say I was overcome with emotion as was my husband is an understatement, I felt a certain kind of energy before, during and after the event.

I had written a poem to be laid at the 'Angels Plot' Where it is believed the children had been buried, I say believed because there are still ongoing investigations taking place in regard to the exact location of the children.

I found out later that there seems to be very little information regarding exactly how many children died at the home. It is believed that there were just shy of *300* babies who died there? *(The exact figure has yet to be established)*

On the day of the commemoration I spoke to several woman who touched briefly on their stories, it took a lot to hold back my tears.

The actual event itself was extremely emotional I could hear in the woman's voices how torn they are not knowing if they will ever know the exact truth.

Some, who had been able to trace their biological mothers had only a short time with them before they passed away, and for many others, they still don't know who their mothers are.

The church and state, have said that they do not hold any records and have very little information for the survivors about their time in the homes.

Of those who approach the nuns that is, those that were still alive at the time were fed lies and or misleading information.

Philomena's son Anthony, also known as *(Michael Anthony Hess)* Was sold to an American couple when he was only three years old, and who as an adult went to the home where he was born to try and find his mother, he too was fed lies by nuns.

I was fortunate enough to meet Philomela who also attends the commemorations every year with her daughter Jane.

She is an extremely gracious woman with a warm heart who has chosen to forgive the nuns, *(something I don't think I could do myself)?*

As Philomena said; *What would be the point of holding on to bad feelings?*

Tuam, SRA, Bethany Home and the Magdalene Laundries are only a few of the many homes/Institutions that existed with the last of them closing their doors in the late *1990s*, I find it astonishing that in the *twentieth*-century they were still running those kind of places.

We have all seen the media, and heard some of the stories of those who had suffered the most horrific of crimes committed by members of the church.

I have talked to some who were illegally adopted and asked what it meant to them to discover that their parents weren't their biological parents.

You know, even if you had a good upbringing, and for many that may not have been the case.

What does matter, is the psychological affects it has when they think that their biological mother gave them up and did not want them in her life?

It isn't until they recovered from the initial shock and come to understand that in fact, they were taken from their mothers arms and sold, perhaps to the highest bidder?

It is basically human trafficking, even more heartbreaking is knowing what some mothers suffered whilst in these homes.

The fact that mothers were ostracised because they became pregnant out of wedlock and that the nuns wanted them to suffer mentally, emotionally and sometimes physically was appalling.

The stigma attached to unmarried mothers along with the reactions of their parents and relatives all in the name of religion is unthinkable, this would never happen in this day and age, or at least I hope not.

To be told that you have sinned then be hidden from society so as not to have communities look down on their families with shame, they were told that they were dirty and some were called whores.

I can't understand and I suppose I never really will? How the church can have that amount of power that so many fear them? I know, it's easy of me to say; *I would not allow the church or any other tell me I have to put my daughter in an institution because she is pregnant out of wedlock'*

Again, perhaps if I had lived during that era, I may have thought differently?

Once the mother entered the home she was instantly given a new name, then she was told the rules and what happens if they are broken.

None of the girls in those homes would know the real name of the other girls, as their identity was completely stripped from them as was their confidence and much more.

The punishment for their sins was manual labour, not only did they have to work for free, many worked right up until the very hour they were due to give birth.

Some of the nuns were extremely harsh, not only mentally, physically and emotionally but they left the woman with no self esteem and for what?

The State paid nuns around ten shillings per head towards looking after the children, yet, they were found to be emaciated by the authoritative figures who called to the homes to inspect them.

If the girls wanted to leave the homes it could have cost around €4000 maybe €5000 in todays money. So the rich girls could buy their way out while the poor girls had to stay and work for free.

The actual figure may never be known as that will remain in the box of secrets held by the Vatican.

Industrial schools were no different in their treatment and in my opinion very racist, also run by religious orders, it has been said that black children were often scrubbed red raw no doubt because of their colour.

Many from Industrial schools were sexually abused for years then basically kicked out when there was no more use for them, or was it because they were too old, no more abuse could take place for fear it would become public knowledge?

Many woman passed through the doors of the Magdalene Laundries too, working their hands to the bone (Free labour) and to be treated with such hatred, yet the church continue to preach we should love everyone equally, they had/have broken that commandment many times over.

The biggest question I ask myself is why has there been no justice? Why was it allowed to happen?

Why are they still refusing to hand over documentation to the very children now adults who were stripped of their identity? What else are they hiding?

Every individual connected to those homes have the right to know their roots, to have the necessary information in relation to their biological mothers and or families dead or alive.

It was during this first visit to SRA, I discovered that the money paid for the children who were adopted was called, *'A Donation'*.

I mean seriously? That in itself tells me there is so much more going on here they don't want people to know.

After the commemorations I went back to the hotel, it was very hard to switch off and go to sleep that night.

My mind was preoccupied with the days events thinking of the stories I had heard from some of the survivors, and that there would be a long road ahead.

Why are the church so powerful? I know that we are talking about institutions here but the power they hold has for whatever reason an influence over a multitude of sectors around the world.

There are several documentaries which I have watched since my return from SRA, many stories I've read that involve the church and clergy from around the globe.

I have had people say to me; Why are you bothering with all this nonsense? You know it's all lies?

Well, actually, I tell them; *No it's absolutely not lies, do people think that all those who suffered from different countries got in a room and decided to tell very similar and often the same stories?* I can't think of any reason why so many people would want discredit the church that badly, that they would want to make it up.

Then I get people saying; Well, that's Catholics for you they are known for their abuse.

Again, I have to correct them by letting them know that it isn't just about the Catholic church, its many religions that are involved in similar or the same crimes.

To think that now we still have that sectarianism is shocking, the world is pretty messed up.

I was supposed to visit Tuam, Galway on this particular trip but with stopping at various places along the way we ran out of time, so had to head back to Tipperary.

This was when I had a passing thought about writing a book, about my thoughts and experiences at the mother and baby home commemorations, assuming I would visit many others on other visits.

After three days in Tipperary, it was time for me to travel back home to Scotland.

After a few days back home that was when I found myself wondering about my feeling towards the Catholic church? I stopped going to mass for a while until I could figure it all out.

So many people are now taking to family heritage sites while creating their family tree, there are many survivors and most likely their biological parents doing the same hoping and praying that their families will eventually find them.

Those of us who have grown up believing, that our parents are our biological parents only to discover they or perhaps one of them *(In my case)* Isn't a biological parent, live with a heavy heart and the need to find the missing piece that makes them feel complete.

No one will ever know unless they have experienced it, what a heavy burden it is to carry, not to mention the heartache surrounding the outcome, so imagine what it must be like for the survivors and their biological parents?

The saddest part of this story is the sorrow that some of the natural mothers are suffering if they have not or cannot tell their families, or had to take that heartbreak to their grave.

This is were I ask you the reader of this book to support the survivors, talk about it with others and yes, even talk about it to the congregation, the more people who understand and support the survivors the better chance they have of a resolution.

Nowadays thankfully, we have DNA Testing which is a good thing even though some may not think so.

I can understand the pain some may feel when they have their results back, especially, if it turns out their father is or was a priest.

The first time I knew about this was reading an article in a newspaper which read as follows.

DNA-TESTING SPARKS PRIEST ALLEGATIONS.
By Sarah Ward

Internet DNA-testing sites have led to a wave of adults discovering that they were fathered by Catholic priests, and banished to Scotland, it has been claimed.

The Catholic Church in Scotland has **admitted** it has no idea how many priests in Scotland have fathered children.

Campaigners claim kids were sent to Scotland from Ireland and England as a way of keeping them hidden from communities which may find out about their parentage.

Founder of campaign group 'Coping International' *Vincent Doyle* said; *"We are supporting eight Scottish people".*

Eight may seem like a small number to many, but for eight people their lives have been hugely affected.

(Copy inserted on next page)

DNA-testing sparks priest allegations

BY **SARAH WARD**

INTERNET DNA-testing sites have led to a wave of adults discovering that they were fathered by Catholic priests and then banished to Scotland, it has been claimed.

The Catholic Church in Scotland has admitted it has no idea how many priests in Scotland have fathered children.

Campaigners claim kids were sent to Scotland from Ireland and England as a way of keeping them hidden from communities which may find out about their parentage.

Founder of campaign group Coping International Vincent Doyle said: "We are supporting eight Scottish people. Eight may seem like a small number to many, but for those eight people their lives have been hugely affected."

We can only imagine the pain of those individuals who had made this discovery, and perhaps there are others yet to discover they were also fathered by priests.

They are the very people we are meant to trust, who teach the word of God and tell us we are protected by our faith in God and them.

I have read several letters sent to individuals in connection with adoptions, I have written just two here, for privacy reasons I am unable to include the actual letters.

Letter 1.

Dear Mr & Mrs xxxx

We have received a very nice letter from your priest, we are very pleased that you persevered in your application, so I think we will be able to give you a baby.

Kindly let me know by return post if possible what age baby you would be interested in?

At the moment we have two lovely boys who were with very great difficulty taken back from Protestant homes in England, both have really good backgrounds.

Don't delay in writing as there is a very great demand for the children at the moment.

God and Mary be with you.

My thoughts!

What strikes me about this letter is the 'Great Demand for Children' Don't get me wrong I'm all for little children being adopted in situations were necessary and under normal legal terms.

However, who really was in demand here? The other thing that I don't quite understand is the two little boys supposedly had a really good background, yet, with great difficulty? They had to be taken back from **Protestant** homes? Aren't we all supposed to be Christians who have been taught to love one another?

Letter 2.

Dear Mrs xxxx

We got your letter and would like you to think more about the adoption of a two year old girl.

We had a wonderful reference from your priest and we think you should take a baby over six months.

For one reason, the baby would be brought up just as you would bring up your own child and a child of two years has been in the institution too long to fall into your ways.

Another thing is the better class girl has to leave here quickly so as not to be detected in her sorrow and so the better class child will be younger, all this thought out would convince you more of taking a young child.

Now at the moment we have a very nice little girl xxxx xxxx who was born on xxxx and is now almost xxxx years old, she is of good background and very intelligent, if you care to have this child you will need to let me know by return post as we have very high demand for children.

Again my thoughts!

What I take from letter 2 is how demanding the nuns seemed to be, they were so fast at getting children out of those homes as soon as they could. *(Kind of made me think of a conveyer belt)*

There also seemed to be an element of forcing of male or female children? Maybe I'm wrong?

The term used in this letter, 'Better Class Girl' *I mean?* A child should NOT ever be thought of as better class to other children.

So did they class some children as 'Non-Better Class'? It does make me wonder? And imagine if this type of letter fell into the hands of the said child?

On a happier note I have been given permission by *Joseph Rice Jrgemmae* to include a copy of a note he had put to the SRA Group on Facebook.

My dear partners from Sean Ross Abbey...

With the US holiday of thanksgiving, I wanted to share with all of you what I was most thankful for in the year of *2019*, I was reunited with my natural mother in Ireland.

I was adopted from SRA sometime back in *1954* at the age of twenty months and taken to St Louis in the US. *(Much like Philomena's son)*

My adoptive parents were told that my mother, was a *nineteen* year old girl who had got pregnant and stayed with me at SRA from birth, this will be of interest later.

My parents were always very honest with me in telling me that I was adopted and sharing with me as much as they knew, including giving me the birth certificate and adoption papers when I was old enough to understand.

I never had much of a yearning to find my mother, but did become more curious as I got older.

My adopted sister Peggy *(Also a member of the site)* Had encouraged me to try and find her and after a couple of vague attempts I finally decided to take definite action in the summer of xxxx.

Peggy and I contacted Ger, *(She had already done so much for Peggy)*

Within a few weeks Ger's people on the ground in London had found my mothers marriage licence *(Not to my father)* and shortly thereafter they found a birth certificate for a daughter.

I found out my mother was still alive and living in Dublin, I was given her address and was able to bring up the picture of her house on the internet.

With a bit of nervousness I wrote my mother a one page letter telling her of my reason to believe that she was indeed my natural mother, giving her a brief description of my life.

I also invited her to communicate but did make it clear that I would not pursue this if she was not interested.

I included some photographs of myself from infancy to the present, I also gave her my address and email.

Around two months later, *(Yes, it took that long for my letter in spite of paying xxxx for a faster delivery)*

I heard from her son, my new brother, he emailed and said that my mother was 'Over the moon' with delight and eager to talk to me to tell me what happened.

I called at an agreed time and we talked for over an hour, this is were the story gets more interesting.

My mother never stayed at SRA and had no idea what it was when I mentioned it in my letter to her.

She had given birth to me in a hospital in Dublin, because she was working and poor, she put me into a care facility where she paid over half her wages to the nuns to take care of me. *(Not SRA)*

My mother, and her sister would ride their bikes to the facility every day after work to see me.

Finally, she could no longer afford the care, so she tearfully signed me over to *Sister Barbara* from SRA for adoption.

She had been told that there was already an American family waiting for me.

This was a lie, it would be close to a year before I had been adopted and of course my adoptive parents were lied to as well with the tale of a pregnant girl having delivered me while staying in SRA under the 'Good Nuns Care'

My mother and I had many phone conversations, In August of that the year *2019* I went to Ireland to meet her and the rest of my siblings, *(Her husband had passed)*. I have four living sisters and a brother, they immediately embraced me and I had a great time with them, along with the extended family.

They even saw to it that my mother and I visited SRA, and the care facility that she was forced to put me in for my first year.

It was very moving for both of us as were many other events shared on that trip.

My siblings tell me that my mother never forgot me and always wondered where I was.

With every year around my birthday, she would become melancholy and they would urge her to try and find me.

But she had no idea where I was, only that I was taken to America.

My mom, *(Yes I call her mom)* Told me that when she opened the mailbox and saw that letter from America, she knew that it had to be me.

I am truly grateful and many thanks to Ger and her angels for coordinating all of this.

This, has been something for which I am truly thankful on this thanksgiving.

Joe.

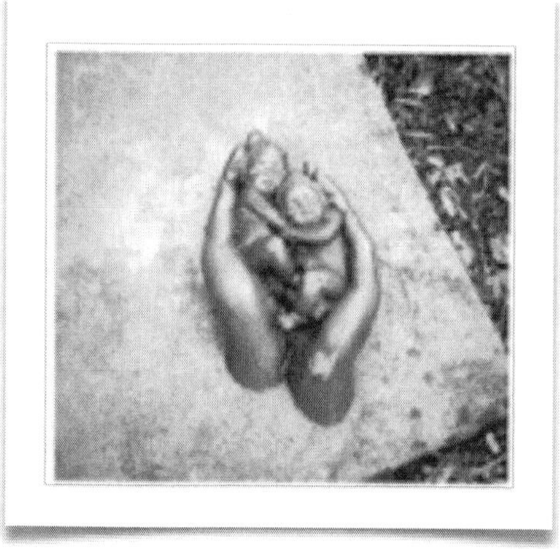

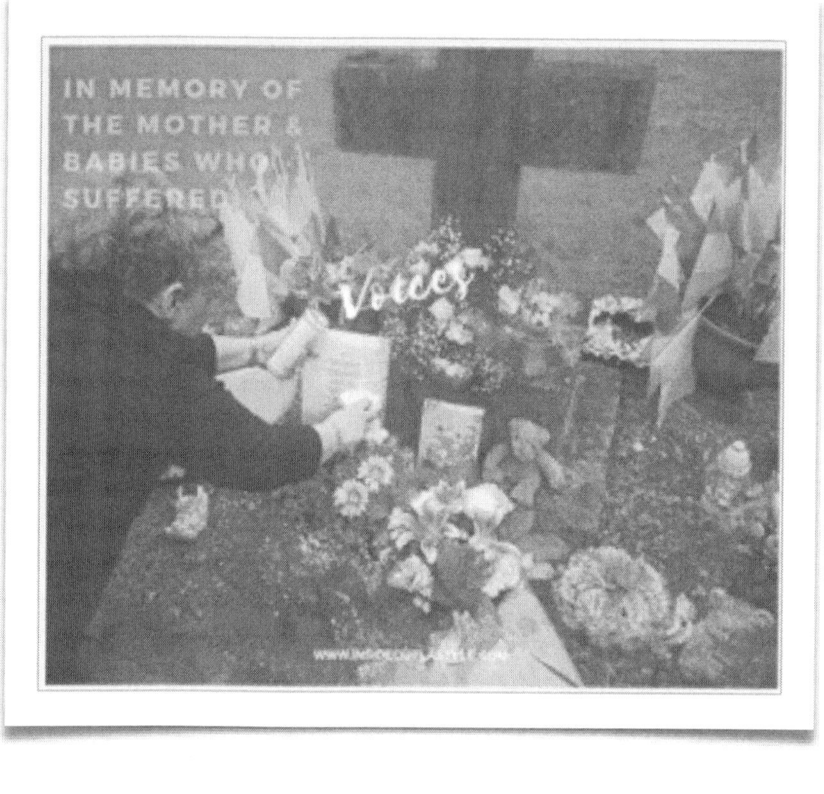
IN MEMORY OF
THE MOTHER &
BABIES WHO
SUFFERED
Voices

That message from Joe is just one of many who have had a happy outcome, there are of course, so many who haven't for various reasons had that happy outcome.

Sadly for some, it was too little too late, as they discovered that their natural mothers had already passed having taken their secrets to the grave.

Some mothers were never given the answers they needed to find their children, or the children came looking and were never given the answers.

And for what, all for monetary gain, a secret the church never wanted to come out, because no matter how you dress it up that is the truth plain and simple.

When you take into account the number of children adopted, all over the world we are talking many millions of pounds and, dollars.

The big question is; Where is all the money? What did they do with it? And why are they not paying for all the investigations if they are supposed to be ashamed of the past? Why not rectify the problems of the past, they wonder why people are falling away from the church?

COMMEMORATIONS 2017

Myself and husband Jerry with Philomena Lee *2017*
Sean Ross Abbey

ENTRANCE TO THE ANGELS PLOT

Inscription;

This memorial garden is dedicated to the babies and infants who died in Sean Ross Abbey and are buried here, May they from their place in heaven pray for us who loved on earth, Jesus said let the children come to me

Where the nuns are buried, such a shame they couldn't have marked the children's burial area as they have their own.

The Angels Plot

VOICES

Those voices you heard inside your head,
Were cries of children waiting to be heard,
Beneath the earth is where we lay,
All this time from that fateful day.

Discarded like trash not a care in the world,
Cold hearts they had, were we that troubled?
Our mothers, heartbroken they were,
The pain they suffered too much to bare.

They said they were unaware,
Now you tell me how is that fair?
Is it enough just to say a prayer?
Our families hearts they cannot repair.

they turned a blind eye that you can be sure,
That blind eye they cannot restore,
They should hang their heads in shame,
They all must share the blame.

Where was their faith? Where was their love?
too soon they sent us to heaven above,
God did not want it this way,
It was their rules that took us that day.

So now we have been found we ask of you this,
admit your sins and take us from this darkness,
Let our families heartbreak cease,
Only then will we rest in peace.

Written in 2017 My first visit to SRA & The Angels Plot

COMMEMORATIONS 2018

I was back at SRA in July *2018* for the commemorations, this was the same year that the survivors and committee unveiled the bench and plaque in memory of the mothers and babies.

It was a warm sunny day which made the unveiling that little bit more special.

The commemorations are a little sombre for those connected to the SRA, it's also a day of reflection and coming together with all who are connected to these Institutions and for most if not all still waiting for answers.

The event is held on the first Sunday of July every year, the day before *(Saturday)* The committee hold a meeting to update any news and progress for the year.

Then on the Saturday evening everyone gathers for a meal and catch up in the function room of the Racket Hall Hotel.

This event gets bigger each year and trust me if it wasn't for the commitments that some can't change the event would be so much bigger.

You have to remember, many of the children, *(Now adults)* Were shipped and or flown to far flung places, such as Australia, USA, Canada, etc., So you can now imagine Just how big the commemorations would be if everyone could make it.

My wish, is that those who read this book, and those who have only just come to learn of the situation that many survivors have been fighting for, will come together in supporting them for justice, for their right to be recognised as human beings with feelings, for their right to know where they came from and for their right to have their loved one's recognised and buried with not only dignity but to have their names displayed in a place that will bring peace to all.

Myself, Jerry and Philomena at the plaque which reads

In Memory of
The Mothers & Babies Home
Sean Ross Abbey
Roscrea
July 1st 2018

The unveiling of the bench *2018*

Teresa Collins & Michael Donovan

The Conference room at the Racket Hall Hotel where we have an update on the Saturday and a meal in the evening.

COMMEMORATIONS 2019

Another commemoration and another year of waiting and needing to fill that void suffered by the survivors, when if at all will that void be filled?

I have briefly gone over what I managed to find online in regards to the various interim reports and even I find it hard to get my head around all the gobildy-gook *(Pardon the expression)* I know, that some of the information even for me is quite hard to understand being that I have no connection *(That I know of)* other than supporting the cause of those suffering/survivors but even I get rather frustrated at the length of time it has taken, is taking to see justice done.

Its hard to put into words the emotion in the faces and voices of those still looking for answers, hearts are breaking and will continue to do so until this is resolved.

From the information I'm reading I can't help but feel that things keep getting put off while every excuse under the sun is being given NOT to pursue the church or the state for past atrocities committed.

Why though Has the church got such a care less attitude or should I say the Vatican? I do shout a lot about the corruption that is going on around the world, the Government, Institutions and so many more but none have such a powerful influence as the church.

The secrets that are held and buried, some of which haven't been uncovered yet, nobody can do anything to bring them to account.

So far we are waiting for the latest interim report to come out which is supposed to be Feb/March 2020 I believe.

What will be in this report, shall there be more covering up of information? Yes, I said it, Covering up! I am being absolutely honest when I say that I truly believe there is so much that is being withheld for fear of a public outcry?

However time will tell, its like most things that happen in life, we will only be told what they want us to know, and i'm not only referring to the church and state here.

2019 commemorations was also attended not only by those who come most years, but also some of the survivors from TUAM which was very nice to see, and made it a little more emotional for me, the fact that they travelled up from Galway, to be there showed, just how dedicated all the survivors are in remembering those who are no longer with them, and that they are all in this together.

I arrived on the Friday with the usual get-together for drinks etc, this year though my husband Jerry wasn't in attendance due to being diagnosed with that dreaded word Cancer back in Nov *2018.*

I actually wasn't going to go myself as he had just had his operation in June and was waiting for his next nine weeks of Chemotherapy, but he insisted I go so that at least one f us was there.

I must add, so many had asked how he was and said they were keeping Jerry in their prayers. Those who know us pretty well now were really concerned for him and that helped me a lot.

Needless to say Jerry was so humbled to have had so many send him regards.

Left to right: Susan, Ger and Barbara from USA

One side of the Angels Plot

Another side of the Angeles Plot which included some of the Tuam survivors

OPENING OF THE BIG HOUSE

On 6 October *2019* we returned Sean Ross Abbey as for the first time in Irish history the doors to the former mother and baby home would be opened to the survivors.

The new owner Tony Donlan who bought the abbey earlier in the year was so kind to welcome those connected to the home.

Teresa Collins, born in the home in *1963*, and Michael Donovan who worked as a Gardner at SRA back in the *1980s* made all the arrangements for that special day.

The days event brought people from Scotland, England and Ireland many of whom told their stories, they hugged each other with an emotional embrace, everyone had some connection to the very home where their mothers gave birth to them.

Also in attendance was the author of *'Republic of Shame'* Caetain Hogan, for those who haven't already read her book it is available on Amazon.

Eamon O'Dwyer from Tipp FM was there to interview many of the visitors and hear their own accounts of SRA.

As far as I am aware, the former nuns house will become a cookery school in the near future.

Tony was very obliging to talk to those who are connected to SRA and will continue to support the yearly visits, he said; *He will be happy to help in any way during future commemorations.*

The whole event took around four maybe five hours, once inside the house there was an element of nostalgia even for me, I think I was initially in shock at how pristine the house was, the Axminster carpets were spotless not a mark to be seen anywhere.

That in itself brought me much sadness, knowing that so many woman had scrubbed and cleaned that home yet were treated so badly for they're so called sins.

The corridors leading to the dining hall were cold and if I might say quite eerie although not as eerie as the basement were the woman would enter the maternity rooms. *(Where they would give birth)*

Still pinned to the walls were the telephone numbers and extensions for doctors, social workers and so many more.

Whilst looking round the house we left no room unturned or at least I thought we didn't until Jerry told me about another room he found in the basement which had around a dozen engraved stones, he took some photos for the book and I'm glad he did because this was one room I didn't manage to get to.

The one that stood out for me was the one you will see on the following page, this particular engraving/quote actually made me cry because although the words are that relating to our lady, it is quoting mothers and speaks for itself, yet, the individuals involved in selling the children clearly didn't think so.

Once finished in the house we got chatting to several people with most still feeling very emotional, then later some of us went on to have some food and drinks and a relaxed chat about the days events.

Photo Credit: PJay Wright

The group standing at the front of the house for the local newspaper

Left to right: Jerry McCool, Teresa Collins & Michael Donovan

The fireplace in the main room

The detail on the ceiling lights are pretty remarkable

The photograph below I took of Mary Keating in the main room

Mary and I were the only two in the room and when I saw her sitting with the piano behind her, I thought it would be a very poignant photo to have in the book

Mother

Our mother is the most delicate of all,
She knows more of paradise than angels can recall,

She is not only beautiful but passionately young,
Playful as a kid yet wise as one who has lived long.

Her love is like the rush of life,
A bubbling, laughing spring,

That runs through all liquid light,
And makes the mountain sing.

She is at once the sea and shore,
Our freedom and our past,

With her we launch our darling ship,
Yet, keep the things that last.

These are just but a few of the plaques in the basement, there were around twelve in all.

Teresa talking with Eamon O'Dwyer of Tipp FM

TERESA'S STORY

My name is Teresa O'Connor (Doyle) I was born and raised at number *12 Haughton Place, in New Ross Co Wexford.*

My mother's name was Bridget Doyle (Cullen) she was born and raised in Byrans town Foulksmill also Co Wexford, and my father was Patrick Robert Doyle. Born and raised at number *2* Nunnery Lane, New Ross Co Wexford.

My father was married twice, first to Stasia Power on *4 Feb 1935* in Glenmore, Co Killkenny his best man was John Payne and Bridget Power was bridesmaid.

I am unsure if there were any children from his marriage to Stasia who passed away between the years *1935* and *1937.*

Dad then married my mother Bridget Cullen on *4 May 1939* at St Aiden's Church, Clongeen their first born child was Patrick on *27 July 1939* then on *14 August 1940* came Annie also known as Nancy.

James was born on *26 October 1941* but sadly passed away a month later on *26* November.

Bridget also known as Bridie was born on *1 April 1943* then came along Robert on *2 November 1945*.

Maryanne also known as Maureen was born on 26 November *1946,* next came Catherine also known as Kathleen on *25 January 1948* then we had William on *15 June 1949* then myself *8 November 1950.*

Before my first birthday baby John was born but died around *October 1951* then in *September 1952* Joseph was born and died on *26 October 1952*.

Thomas and Angela the twins were born on *26 October 1953* they lived only a few months then passed away in the December.

I do remember them in the bed with my mum they had bandages around their hands to stop them scratching their tiny faces.

Mother had four other sons John, Joseph, Denis and James who all died young between *1954-1957*.

Then in *1956* martin was born and in *1958* came Richard, on *30 May 1964* Geraldine was born to my sister Maureen, my mother took over in raising Geraldine who would then be known as our sister.

I was thirteen and a half when myself and brother William were given the job of looking after her as she was a few months old. Martin aged eight and Richard six were the villains, all our older brother and sisters had gone to England to find work.

I went to St Joseph's national school, Michael St New Ross it's strange how the mind works, there is a lot I can't remember but I do remember my first day at school which was on *1 June 1955*.

I knew the date because I got my school records to prove the good shepherd convent in Cork wrong on the dates they had on their records.

Most of the kids were upset, I can remember I was sitting down at the back of the class were I kept looking towards the door until my mother left.

I can still visualise my mother standing there with her full length tweed coat and visibly upset.

I actually got on very well at school and I hardly ever missed a day, although on occasion I did skip school with my friends.

I loved the Irish lessons but they never really went into much explanation of the translation which was not very helpful but I went on to the sixth class and was signed in to do a third year then that ended when dad sent me away.

Mother must have suffered a great deal of heartbreak in her life trying to rear and provide for us all and burying six of her children, it seems in those days a lot of children dies, heaven knows why.

My mum lived around ten miles from her own parents and family, it was hard for her to get out there what with so many kids but believe it or not we went there on an ass and cart.

What a journey you would not be long there until it was time to come back home before the dark of night fell.

We used to love our trips to granny Cullen's house they were really lovely people, so kind and caring, they always made us welcome and we loved having some of granny Cullen's baked brown bread.

She fed us well on the many trips to her home, then on *18 September 1938* my fathers dad died, he was pre deceased by nanny Doyle.

I am unsure when granny Doyle dies as we never knew them, they dies before we were born so there was not much help around for my mum.

Dad worked at the farm labouring before he got a job with New Ross Council, I had many happy memories meeting dad and Jim Holden with their horse and cart collecting household rubbish from door to door around New Ross.

Some years later the council graduated from using the horse and cart to using refuge lorries and dad spent some time on the lorries too.

He then went on to sweeping the streets to eventually working in the council's yards which took him up to receiving his redundancy retirement payment around *1965*.

Dad was very fond of the drink which caused many hardships for my mother, there were a lot of rows over money because many a time she would send me for groceries to Cleary's shop down the town with a note for credit only to be told, 'Sorry tell your mother the other bill has to be paid first'.

It got to the stage were I hated being sent for the shopping and even though I was young I remember the embarrassment,

On the faces of the shop assistants, I felt awful because there were other people present.

I often wondered if any of my older sisters had gone through this before they left home?

I would get home and my mother would be in tears wondering were she would get food from? She was well thought of by the O'Shea's in the Irishtown shop and no matter what she owed they never refused her even though she didn't want to keep asking the one shop for credit all the time.

She shopped at three grocery stores Cleary's, O'Shea's and Mary Jo Coadys in Mary Street.

During hard times, mother often went without to make sure we had enough she was a great baker, she would make at least three brown loaves a couple of times a week and she would boil a lot of fresh beetroot.

She mostly boiled chicken and of course the fish monger Jim Harney lived at the bottom of our lane, we would have fresh fish regularly, Jim knew mum had a big family, he was very generous to us.

Dad done his best he was a hard worker, his downfall on pay day was that he couldn't pass by the pubs but overall he loved us all and he was a good dad.

My dad was very musical and played the accordion, he would play the tin whistle, the mouth organ and the fiddle, he taught himself how to play those instruments.

He had two little dancing masters made of wooden boy, arms and legs with a piece of wire around the neck to control them.

He used to dance them on top of the tea chest board it was great and gave us hours of entertainment, he had many talents during his lifetime.

His brother Martin was killed on *14 September 1915* in the first world war, I proudly hold his medal and army photographs which were presented to my granny and granddad Doyle after his death.

My dad was born in the workhouse on *31 July 1911* and was only five years old at the time of uncle Martin's death.

It must have been an awful time for my grandparents back then with their first born son tragically killed in the war.

I done okay at school, each day after once I had finished my homework, I would go to my grandmother Mrs McDonald who lived at 7 Haughton Place.

I would do her shopping for her she would give me sixpence at the end of the week, I thought a lot of my grandmother.

I would then go to Mrs Freaney's she owned a shop and post office at the top of Haughton Place, I would take buckets of swirl *(Also known as leftover foods)* To the Haughton hospital for her, don't ask me what they done with it? Perhaps they had a farm behind the grounds of the hospital.

All I can remember was the weight and the stench of the buckets. Mrs Freany would not give me money but she gave me a few sweets and the empty ice cream cartons, I would bring them home and get a knife and scrape all the ice cream off the cartons to eat.

I never had the money to buy an ice cream or chocolate, not like the kids of today they will never know what that feeling was like.

I don't know if thats a good thing or a bad thing as it seems to be Christmas every day for some kids.

I had four good friends Kathleen Callaghan, Moira Bulger, Jenny Fanning and Marie Cashin, they all lived in JKL Place, New Ross.

My brother Pat and his wife Mary lived there with their children, Pat was tragically drowned on *12 September 1968*.

I won't ever forget that because I lived here in Clara and mum sent me a telegram which was a heartbreaking time for all the family, especially for his wife Mary and the children who were all very young.

My friends and I would call one another's homes and as we got older we would go to the cinema down town together.

We took part in the plays at the New Ross theatre which we enjoyed very much.

Then one night when Moira and Jenny could not come out Kathleen and I would go into town where she found two pounds, we went to the restaurant area of the cafe and got fish and chips with peas and a drink, it was something we would never have afforded before.

We were so happy, every night when we were in town we would peep through the glass panelled door and see them all stuffing their faces.

Here we were now sitting eating our meal we felt like royalty, when we left the cafe around eight o'clock we would go to the sweet shop on the corner and bought a bag of mixed sweets we were in our glory.

When we went home we didn't tell our parents about it, we were thirteen at the time.

The next day at school Garda Carroll visited each classroom in the school to enquire if anyone had found two pounds the previous night, of course nobody owned up.

He went on to tell us that the two pounds had been lost by an old age pensioner, our one and only night of feeling like royalty turned to sadness.

We could no longer stay silent and we owned up and to be honest I can't remember if our families paid back the two pounds back? Knowing my mum and dad and Kathleen's family they would have paid it back, so the lesson here is to find doesn't mean you have to keep.

We all started flagging lifts to Waterford City to the friends we had down there, we would leave early to get home, we done that about half a dozen times during the school holidays.

As most teenagers do without realising the dangers of a big city at night trying to flag down a lift to get home often which took ages for the four of us and resulting in us arriving home late.

I would always get in trouble for being late because I was supposed to be home by 10pm so when I arrived around eleven, I would get a few clouts with my dad's army belt, and by God it was sore I would be marked for days.

Then came the night we couldn't get a lift so decided to walk home, bearing in mind it was twelve miles from New Ross we had no choice but to walk.

It was in the month of *September 1964* and very dark, we were scared as this had never happened before.

We had walked a few miles of that road and were tired so we thought we would rest behind a wall.

We were freezing cold and all we could think of was what would happen to us once we got home?

I knew my mum and dad would be mad, as soon as it was bright we got back on the road, eventually a bus came along and he gave us a lift.

The driver asked why we were on the road so early? We told him what happened then he gave us a lecture on the danger of what we had done.

At that time we were young and couldn't see the danger, as we approached the Waterford Road in New Ross just going over the bridge when my brothers Pat and Kathleen's brother Eddie spotted us on the bus.

They ran after the bus until it stopped outside Matty Ryan's pub on the quay, Pat grabbed hold of me and said they were out looking for us since midnight.

Robert my brother was also out with Pat looking for us and while they were glad to see us all back safe and well, they fought all the way home with me.

Pat and Robert gave out to me for keeping mum and dad up all night, it was after eight o'clock when we got home, my dad had gone to work in the county council down in Mary Street.

Mum was relieved to see me but gave me a few thumps, she was getting my brother Martin ready for school, Richard was too young for school.

Pat and Robert went off to work in Stafford's mum gave us me breakfast then after Martin went to school she told me to have a wash and because I was so tired told me to go to bed for a while.

Off I went to bed and didn't wake up until Martin got home from school after three o'clock, I remember being sick with worry of dad coming home from work, thinking I was going to get hiding with his army belt.

He eventually got hoe and mum said, 'You're early home tonight' Then Kathleen's dad Ned came into the house.

We were sent upstairs while they were talking, we lay on the bedroom floor with our ears to the ground trying to hear what they were talking about but we couldn't hear anything.

We used to do that whenever mum and dad were arguing about how much he had spent on drink.

After some time mum came into the bedroom and told Martin and Richard to stay there then took me downstairs, she had been crying because her eyes were red.

She explained to me that there was nothing she could do, my father had made his mind up after being advised by the Garda and the nuns that it would be better for me to be sent to the Good Shepherd Convent where I would be educated by the nuns.

He listened to their advice, money was very scarce in our house and mum was not well.

I suppose us not being able to get that lift home meant nothing to us because we were young but mum and dad worried, the five of us had already decided never to thumb a lift to the Waterford Cinema anymore as it was very dangerous.

Back then people like my dad trusted the law and didn't know that the convent was a slaves den.

I thought dad was going to give me a beating and that was why my mother was so upset, nothing could have prepared me for what happened next.

Dad told me to put on my coat, he didn't argue with me he just said; One day you are going to thank me for what I am doing today, that day was *22 September 1964* just before my *fourteenth* birthday.

In *2007* when I got my Magdalen Laundry records it showed dates that were wrong, they said I was taken to the laundry on *28 Jan 1964* and that I was sent home on *21 May 1965*, the records were completely wrong.

I personally feel they had been deliberately written wrong? Their reason because I should have been in the school in the convent, not working.

I had written to the convent to explain they were wrong but they would not change them for me.

I and my family know how long I was there so the fact that they would not change them no longer matters.

I still had no idea what was happening? Until the Garda walked in and said; *Are you ready Mr Doyle?*

I was then led out to the Garda car against my will and put in the back seat. My mum never said goodbye to me, it felt like the bottom had fallen out of my world.

Looking back now I'm sure she was more upset than I was at what was happening.

The only way to describe how I was feeling, it was very sickening I suppose and I felt I wasn't wanted not to mention extremely lonely.

As I looked up toward the bedroom window I could see my brothers martin and Richard they were crying their eyes out at the sight of me being put into the squad car.

I was the one who always looked after them, they were shouting out of the window for my dad to bring me back into the house, but he didn't do it.

Minutes later the car was driving up Irish Town then stopped outside the convent, dad took me up to the big brown door and knocked on it.

It was answered by an oldish nun, we were taken inside and only then did I know what was happening to me.

A senior nun came in and led us into a room were dad had to sign a form given him by mother superior.

She told him I would be educated where I was going, how wrong was she? Or should I call her a *fucking liar?*

She knew well what I would be doing when I got to cork, the slave home for youngsters.

Shortly afterwords dad left the convent, no explanation and no goodbyes and at that very moment I hated my father for what he had done.

I was thinking to myself, 'What have I done that was so bad the he and my mum don't want me anymore?'

You don't just send your children away to a convent without knowing anything about it?

Another nun came and gave me clean cloths and told me I was going for a bath and that after my bath she would explain the procedures of the convent.

I was taken to bedroom and got into bed, the nun took me up tea and sandwiches, it was only five-thirty in the evening.

The nun told me I would be kept in New Ross convent that evening and in the morning be sent to Sundays Well Good Shepherd convent in Cork.

Being young I didn't take in all this conversation with the nun, when she left the room I finished my tea, then fell asleep.

The nun called me around *seven* o'clock to say I had a visitor, I sat up in bed as the door opened, It was my mother.

She had been talking to the nun and telling her that she was taking me home, she told my mother that she couldn't do that as my father had signed the papers and she was unable to reverse that decision.

My mother said to her that she was my mother not the nun and was entitled to take me home.

They were both shouting by this point and I was very upset as I had never heard my mother raise her voice before.

The nun then said to my mother to come back the following morning at ten am to discuss my case further.

Of course what the nuns didn't tell my mother I would be taken to Cork magdalen Laundry.

Six am the next morning a lady by the name of Bernadette McNamara came and took me to Waterford by bus from New Ross before reaching St Mary's Close in Cork.

We walked from the bus stop up the big hill, I kept thinking about my mother and the fact that once she went to see the nun at ten am I would be gone.

It hurt knowing that when I sae my mother the night before leaving Cork how upset she was that she was not able to take me home.

I could tell that my mother was very sad about what had happened to me, mum did tell the nuns that when she returned at ten am the next morning that she would be taking me home with her, sadly she never got that chance.

That morning before leaving I got dressed and went for breakfast, a bowl of cornflakes.

I kept thinking that my father would come before they had the chance to take me away, I kept watching the big clock in the front room but to my disappointment he didn't come.

The reason for that, my father worked for the county council and began work every morning at eight am.

It was the *23 of September 1964* that Bernadette McNamara took me away to Waterford, I can still hear Bernadette knocking on the big knocker on that door, it was answered by an oldish lady who certainly didn't have a smile on her face.

When we got inside the convent the first thing that happened was me being escorted to the head nuns office.

From here, I was handed over to another lady known for distributing the convent uniforms, she was extremely unfriendly and liked to show her authority.

She took me up a winding staircase to where she told me to remove my own cloths.

Others were doing embroidery on handkerchiefs, I was told to introduce myself and by the look on all their faces I pondered for a few minutes before saying my name was taken from me and now they call me Joseph.

As I sat down at the table everyone kept telling me *'Don't go against the ladies in charge'*.

They were in the convent most of their lives some from birth they were called Auxiliary's meaning, nuns without uniforms.

At 8:30pm we would recite the rosary which was something I was used to as mum and dad always said the rosary every evening in our house, we knelt down with great respect at the chairs.

We would be in bed by 9:00pm every night in the convent, it was a very large room with lots of single beds it was always freezing cold and not much bed blankets but you dare not complain, I did which resulted in me always being at war with them.

Next morning we were called around 5:30am to get washed and dressed, we all went into the massive breakfast room where there were several long breakfast tables with a selection of small amounts of cornflakes, porridge, bread, jam and tea.

You could have a choice of one of them, prayers were always said before and after meals.

No one told me what was to come next, we were all taken to a very big room across from the breakfast area.

I thought I was going to school but nothing prepared me for what happened next.

All the girls were used to their chores and rushed to their work places, within the room were rows of ironing boards all fitted in their own cubicles with one girl in each space.

Further up the room was a laundry area and a big roller that was used to press the sheets, bed spreads and blankets.

This was the area I was placed to work in and my Lord you would not be idle for a moment, I will come back to this later.

In another part of the room there were pressers and behind the entrance door into the work area with a pulpit, this is where nuns would take it in shifts to watch over the girls making sure we were doing our work and no talking all day long.

This went on from around *6:30* in the morning until *5:30* in the evening sometimes much later at night.

I won't ever forget the name stamp on the clothing it was the Metropole Hotel Cork.

After a few months working in the laundry where we worked like slaves I was moved to the ironing area where I ironed all day except for dinner break.

I would pile all my finished ironing onto a counter top and other girls would come to collet them.

I a crease was left on any of the ironing they would bring them back for you to re-do them, they had to be perfect.

"That still remains with me today, now at home I hate ironing every time I iron I get emotional half way through, I do my ironing perfectly because the laundry comes to mind, under my breath I curse them".

They would pack the laundry in large cane baskets with lids on them, the work was very hard and you could not complain, some of the nuns were lovely but not all.

Every Saturday was post day, they would call out the names of all the girls who got letters I didn't get letters every Saturday.

It was very down heartening when you didn't receive mail, however, my mum was the only one that ever wrote to me and I loved to get her letters.

Nobody else knew I was in there amazingly not even my family as they were all mostly in the U.K and working.

I was proven right when I eventually got out of there on *21 October 1965*. I came to find out that my mum did write to me every week but they kept a lot of the letters from me, my mum told me when I got home.

I blocked out a lot of what went on at Sundays Well Convent until I started to write my story.

I remember trying to get out by climbing through windows but you didn't have a hope in hell, there were massive high windows and needed a ladder to get out.

There is every chance you would have been killed as the drop was extremely high on the outside, really, it was like a prison as you could not leave on your own accord.

On holy days we would march around the gardens for hours on end praying, when we were out there it was the only time we would see daylight.

There was *three* of us who would plan our escape, *two* of the girls were from Limerick and Galway.

We were at the back of the procession, so we slipped behind the trees and ran down the back where there was a high green gate.

None of us could open it the Gardner seen us then reported us to the nuns.

Our punished was to be locked in the dormitory for two or possibly three days with no food, we were all freezing.

We were not all in the same room, we had very little blankets in there it was a nightmare.

When the others came to bed at night it was great I had company even though we couldn't talk just knowing they were there was comfort, there was always some lady put in charge of each dormitory, it was a lesson learned but not so me as I will explain later in the story of when I approached Mother Mount Carmel as I gave her a piece of my mind. *'I was a rebel, always fought my corner'*

My legs used to pain me badly, standing *six* days a week ironing I often wondered was it because of the time spent slaving away in that institution?

The problems with my neck, arms and legs are a because of the way in which we had to do it, they say that health problems catch up with you later in life as a result of our past lifestyle.

As the months went on I despised my father, I thought; 'If only he could see what we had to do in that place'

My parents didn't know what went on there because we were not allowed to talk about it, not in letters nor visits, not that I got any visits as my parents had no transport and it was a long way from New Ross to Cork.

"I am finding it very difficult to talk about my time in the convent, I didn't have any intentions of including that part of my life in a book" I had spent *thirteen* months of my life in that place and it felt like years.

One day Bernadette who was very good to me said; 'Mother Mount Carmel wants to see you in her office'

When I got there, she told me to sit down, "She was a lovely nun|" She said to me that that I would be going home next day as my father had signed a release form.

I burst into tears because I never thought I would get out of there, to be honest it was very harsh indeed but being nuns you never wanted to condemn them, but the bad ones need to be condemned because they were evil bitches and the good nuns need to be praised.

That evening at tea it was announced that tomorrow we will be saying goodbye to Joseph *(Me)* Then I remember her "saying" Will you stand up Joseph *Three* times she repeated herself and I would not stand up.

Why have you disobeyed me I have asked you *three* times to stand up did you not hear me?

When the nun finished speaking I stood up and said; My name is not Joseph and never has been.

My name is Teresa Doyle, then, there was silence, it was not me being cheeky it was me letting them know that they had no right to take my given birth name from me.

I was christened Teresa, that is my identity and nobody can take that away from me.

That night before bed they all said their goodbyes, I was very happy to be leaving but also sad to leave them behind.

The majority of the nuns were okay, I know that there is a lot of people taking who have court cases against some of the religious orders over all types of abuse that took place in the convents.

I have experienced some but I don't wish to elaborate on it, perhaps education and unpaid slaves. Back then a *fourteen* year old was not very educated to be able to understand why those convents could be run in such a manner as our little minds were equivalent to that of a ten year old today, thank God the kids of today are very bright.

Next morning, I had to work on the ironing until lunch time, I kept telling myself I would never have to see this place again, that date was *21 October 1965.*

Before leaving the convent at *four* o'clock Mother Mount Carmel said she would keep in contact with me by letter.

She was one in a million, Bernadette McNamara took me by bus to Waterford the journey ahead would take hours.

She had brought sandwiches for us to eat along the way and asked me to keep in touch with her by letter which I did along with Betty O'Driscoll.

It was a dark, wet night when we arrived in Waterford at 9:30pm my mother and sister Esther along with my brother in law Jimmy Philpott were there to meet me.

Bernadette shook hands with me and said goodbye, she was going to stay at the Good Shepherd Convent in Waterford that night then travel back to Cork next day.

I remember feeling confused when I stepped into the house, my father was sitting on his armchair, he said; *"Well I hope you have learned lessons"* After he had welcomed me home.

For what Dad? I said? What did I do wrong that you sent me away? Then I said; Why do some children hate their fathers?

There was a look of hurt on his face and at that point I knew I had hurt his feelings.

At that point my mother drew me a slap across the face and told me to respect my father. Looking back, I can honestly say that that episode of my life came between me and my father.

It was years later that dad told me he believed I was going to the Good Shepherd school to be educated that he was assured of that by the nuns.

Then he told me that even though times were hard with mum not able to manage to pay the bills nor put food on the table and even though Martin and Richard were young children, he wasn't able to say it wasn't a good reason to send me away, it was getting harder so the option from the nuns sounded good.

He was very sorry, at that moment I did feel sorry for him to because there were tears in his eyes. I have to say that when I told mum and dad the way that I was treated in cork they wished they had never sent me there.

Dad said that he thought I would get a good education and he believed that nuns did not tell lies.

I know now that mum sent letters of protest to the convent in both New Ross and Cork as well as to the minister of justice of the day.

Both, my brothers were glad to have me home. Esther and Jim finished their tea then went home, I was very tired from the journey and went to bed.

My time in Cork was never spoken again in our home it was as if it had never happened, so I suffered in silence.

A few months later I left home and went to Offaly, for many years I got on with my life kept in contact with Bernadette, Betty and Mother Mount Carmel until their deaths, all died in the past number of years but were good people who treated you humanity.

People may find this hard to believe but even though I kept in contact with all three, at no time did we discuss any of the abuse that went on in the convent.

It was always conversation about present day about my life and my children and them giving me advice.

There was only about *six* people I treasured their letters, read them often and cried. The hardest thing for me was never being able to discuss with anyone my years in the convent.

The first time I was able to talk about it was when I lived in England and I made friends with a cork man who later became an extended member of our family, we thought the world of John Cunningham, he would tell us stories about cork.

One day I asked him if he knew of Sundays Well Convent He said he knew it well and asked how I knew the place? I never answered John but somehow he knew.

One day we were in the Rose and Crown pub and I told him how I new the convent, John was such a soft hearted person, he just held my hand and said; *'Sure it was an experience to put behind me and it probably made me the caring person I am today,'* Perhaps john was right because at that moment I forgave my father and realised he was trying to protect me.

I can honestly say that although it was hard I was not badly treated, to put it in a nutshell things were not great either but I was fortunate enough to stand up for myself.

For what was right the majority of them would back off at the first sign of trouble in the room, but as time went on some started to do what I doing and stood up for themselves too.

On the *19 Feb 2013,* We the magdalen children got an apology from our Taoiseach Edna Kenny on behalf of the state.

Ever since I'm very emotional at times but the apology was welcomed, I was so delighted with it and then they set up what became known as 'The Judge Quirke Enquiry' Into the magdalen laundries.

The decision to compensate us for the work we done in the laundry, the amount that we would get would depend on the time spent in the laundry.

The survivors were asked to gather their records, I was lucky that I had mine from the claim I made from the Redress Board that I had made in *2005,* on the ground of my loss of education.

I had a solicitor and barrister provided by the state and in my book worked on behalf of the state to give as little as possible.

I was not allowed to go in and speak to the redress board, only the legal team could go in and speak on my behalf which was a disgrace as in their statements they had made mistakes.

After half an hour they came out and said that the redress board would not budge they offered only two and a half thousand fro the loss of my education.

As those years in Ireland children finished school at *fourteen,* the legal team thought that it was a reasonable offer, they asked me to think about it.

I told them I didn't need to think about their offer it's not coming out of their pockets, Oliver my husband was with me and

I asked him what he thought? He said; The decision was mine and of course he was right.

I told my legal team, *No way*, I could have made something of my life if I had the education instead I was made a slave.I told them to go back in and tell the redress board to stick their measly offer and make me a decent one.

They came back out and the offer was now €5000 I declined again.

Third time lucky, they then offered me €10.500 and another €141.00 for travel costs, so I excepted that offer.

It took from *2005-2007* To receive my cheque from the board of education in Tullamore.

I kept a copy of my cheque as a souvenir, bear in mind my records from the convent were wrong they only paid me from *28 January 1964 to 21 May 1964.*

Four months even though they had my school records to prove when I went into the convent in the Irish town New Ross *22 Sept* on for an overnight stay then went to Sunday Wells Cork on *23 Sept 1964* and came home on *21 October 1965.*

My sister Esther wrote them a letter and told them this as she, her husband Jimmy and my mother met me in Waterford from the Cork bus.

So now in *2013* I gathered all my paperwork together and sent it to the department of justice in Dublin, this time I handled it all myself, no solicitors, I had the same problem again.

After *several* months they wrote to me and said I had only four months in the convent and that I was claiming for *thirteen* months.

I wrote them a good letter and asked who was in the convent them or me? I was not likely to forget it.

I told them I had written to the nuns and asked them to amend my records but as not many of them were still living and those who were, were now very old and could not remember me.

They told me they would only pay me for *four* months at €10.500 I told them I would not except it and would I would get a letter rom the nuns in new Ross.

They wrote me a very good letter and could prove I was in school class on the last day in *Sept 1964*.

That was great because now the justice office would have to take that into consideration, the only other proof that we had which was my sisters Esther's letter as my mum was dead, she passed away on *31 Dec 1994* (Rip) So they didn't except my sisters letter, then I was offered *eight* months compensation at €16.500.

My health has deteriorated after fighting with them for a year, I suffered with stress so I excepted the payment but swore I would fight for my other €5000 When Mrs Farrell Solicitor from O'Connor Square Tullamore was signing up my paperwork she added to the forms that I was not happy being left short of my €5000 There was no more I could do I had excepted their offer and received the cheque in *July 2014*.

100

We bought ourselves a *2013* plate car, paid off our credit union and with the €*74.00* left I took my husband for an Indian meal in Tullamore.

At last I had received payment for all the work I had done even though I had been left short for the time spent in the convent *thirteen* months not *four*.

I had decided to appeal to the Ombudsman unfortunately Mr Nasty turned me down, he believed them not me, abused all over again by state bodies, I will fight this until the end.

In *June 2017* There was an event held for all the magdalene survivors by Dublin remembers the magdalen's which was hosted by Norah Casey Ambassador.

Claire McGetterick and Dr katherine O'Donnell and Maeve O'Rourke On the first night we had a *five* course meal in the mansion house with many of Irelands top musicians playing.

Christy Moore, Daniel O'Donnell, Philomela Begley, and the Irish dancers River Dance and so many more it was an amazing night.

Speeches were made in which Minister Charlie Flanagan gave his apologies to the magdalen survivors. He went on to say that all the ladies who were left short with payments under the redress scheme would get paid.

A group had gone to the Ombudsman office to complain and after a few years complaining they decided in our favour.

They could have done that with me back in *2014* and made life easier. So we soon received forms from the department of justice to be filled in on behalf of Mary O'Toole, I filled mine in and sent it back thinking at last this will all be over and I can put all the stress behind me.

Low and behold she wrote back asking me to remember all the gils names who were in the Sunday Well Magdalen Laundry after *May 1965*.

She wanted my sister Esther to remember more than she could *fifty-two* years before, I wouldn't mind but I sent her my school records and on them it stated that my last day in school in *1964*.

Every day from Jan until *Sept 1964* was marked in the school roll book. I was present in school with the exception of a few days that I was sick or on holidays.

The nuns even wrote an explanatory letter for my time at school and that when I never went back to school after the *12 Sept 1964* that nobody had told them where I had gone.

The bottom line is the convent records stated I was in the Good Shepherd Convent Sundays Well Cork from *28 January 1964 until 21 May 1964*. That was impossible, as I had been in St Josephs School Mary Street New Ross.

Whenever a new person came into the slave house of Sundays Well Cork we would be introduced to each other but they didn't understand that we were not allowed to talk, if we were fond out to be talking we were sent to the cold dormitory and left there to go hungry having no supper.

With all the stories that had been told of the treatment in the magdalen laundries through the media and RTE, the Government selected a senior council lady by the name of MO who carried out the work of paying the those who had been left short in the redress payment.

She had no idea what went on and the stress we have been suffering all over again just to get the money that was due to us.

Nobody including myself had our own name as we all had our identity taken from us.

I had a letter delivered to me asking for permission to look into my revenue affairs, I had signed it and until at the time of this story waiting to hear back.

I had called the justice office and asked AO what the idea was of senior council MO looking for those details?

She told me that it would help MO establish if I was in the magdalene laundry and for how long, why she couldn't take my word for it I don't know? She had seen the magdalen records, school records etc, It showed that they were proved wrong.

I find it amazing how she MO would assume that I would lie about such a thing, and that we had been treated so disgracefully whilst in the laundry and after.

I have a friend who lives locally who was also in Wexford Summerhill Convent, I called her and asked if she too had a form to sign to allow them to look into her revenue information? She said no.

When my friend was claiming her redress payment I helped her get her payment and have copies of all her paperwork. The convent papers only show the date she went in not the date she came out.

They had down that she was *fourteen* years old, so we got copies of her school records which proved the nuns to be lying again.

To get our payments back in *2014* we had to sign away our rights and promise not to take any legal action against them on the condition they would give us our payments and enforce justice JQ's recommendations.

However, they have broken their own agreement because the judge said that all magdalene survivors were to receive a health card equivalent which was issued to the Hepatitis C group of people.

We only got an enhanced card, 'Not great for what we suffered the word equivalent means the same, "Equal."

I had written several letters to LV, SH, and M.Mc, even the transport minister SR. We thought with his group holding the balance of power he might help us? How wrong was I? He didn't want to know and referred it to RG Who hadn't even bothered to contact us.

I will keep going I know my rights, I don't keep in good health I suffer from Fibromyalgia, Cervical Rib Syndrome and Atrial Fibrillation of the heart but they don't care.

Their sorries were meaningless they were only vote catching, but Karma is ok.

All I have to say is for many years this took over my life, it took my energy and whether they give me my €*5000* I was left short they had *five* months of slavery from me.

I don't look up to priests, nuns or high society anymore they are meaningless to me, but I don't hate them either as to hate would be very wrong and would achieve nothing.

I forgive easily for the things that I wasn't responsible for, and that includes my father, who was unaware of what was actually going on in those places.

He believed the priests and nuns and anyone religious, but he soon found out the truth.

The *50s, 60s* and *70s* were bad times in Irish society, the state,and the churches of the day were all involved in what was happening. The poor girls who had children in the laundries many of whom were fathered by priests or Garda, they were the real victims for they had their children taken/stolen by the nuns and sold for a vast amount of money to American's which is unforgivable.

I now know just how much my parents were lied to by the nuns, they told my parents I would have a good education, the only education I learned was how to use an iron and not even on an ironing board but a hard piece of old timber.

The laundry was locked away in my memory until *2013* when we got our apology which was given by EK FG Taoiseach.

I think all survivors were grateful for that, I will carry on as of and from *Jan 2019*, fighting the state for the *€5000* with interest and my HAA Card that is still due to me.

No one will ever sit on my shoulder again, there is no room for them I am now and have been since my *70th* more than able to fight my own corner. I do a lot of work in Clara, I help those who are unable to help themselves, especially young people. I'm happy to help them.

My education is the University of life, and I don't look back but to be truthful the magdalene laundry, Sunday Well Cork is embedded in my mind it would be impossible for me or any survivor to erase that part of out lives from our memory.

In a nutshell it was the worst experience of my life and I would not wish it on my worst enemy. I don't look up to nuns, priests or any high society anymore they are meaningless to me, however, I don't hate them either.

To hate would be wrong, it won't do our health any good as nothing ever came from bitterness, it eats you up like a cancer.

Good riddance to Sunday Well Cork, those who committed those atrocities have god to answer to.

The last time I seen that convent it had been burned possibly by those who purchased it as they wanted to build flats or houses on the site, despite the fact that there is young Nellie's grave in there.

Nellie was a seven year old child who died of a crippling disease, she was left there by her father to be minded by the nuns as he was a seaman, he sadly drowned on one of his trips.

Little Nellie remained in the convent to be cared for until she died.

I took my children there in *1985* they were shown little Nellie's room with her tiny bed, Mother Bridget gave my *two* children books of Nellie's story which was very sad.

Apart from Nellie's grave there are many good nuns buried there at the back of the convent.

I won't look back in anger, so when you read this remember these were dark days in Ireland that the Government would rather forget.

Children were sold, the babies in the tuam Mother and Baby Home and all over Ireland most did not have a dignified burial. May God bless you all.

Teresa O'Connor

Clara Offaly.

MARY'S STORY

Mary Buckley also known as Betty from Clare, Co Offaly a *fifty-three* year old woman, married with *seven* children *four* of whom still lived at home, she herself *one* of *seven* children.

What you are about to read is an account of the psychiatric medical report.

Betty has asked that I include the report in this book, she herself still finds it very hard to talk about those dark time in her life. The following is extracts of the report, I have omitted the names of doctors, solicitors and the recommended treatment and prognosis for privacy reasons.

Dated 2003

Betty had been placed in the Convent of Mercy Summerhill, Wexford. at the age of *eleven* and remained in the institution until she was almost *fifteen*.

Her father died when she was almost *six* years of age, she barley remembers him but he was sick as long as she knew him.

Her mother was to remarry but her stepfather didn't want to have the responsibility of caring for his wife's existing family so Mary and her sister Bridie were put into care.

The boys were "Done for" at the time and the youngest child remained with the mother until she remarried. Betty had horrible memories of her time spent in the convent of mercy.

She described her life as poor and disadvantaged before she was placed there. Her mother was forced out of work to wash for the farmers in order to support the family.

Her older sister Nancy took over many household tasks and Betty had mixed relationships with her mother, Life was no frills and there was not a lot of time for niceties.

She was physically and emotionally abused in the convent of mercy receiving no education in the convent, she had been put to work right away in the laundry and often worked a *twelve* hour days.

The work was backbreaking, she was the youngest 'inmate' in the institution, she did complete her confirmation before going to Wexford and that was the end of her education.

The laundry catered for the local hotels and townspeople, the emphasis was on religion and work.

The physical conditions were very grim, she described the dormitories as lonesome, now and then Betty wet the bed and would sleep in wet sheets sooner than tell the nuns.

She had been beaten up to *twice* a week and was whipped by the nuns with a leather. Betty would often be locked in a small hot press for hours at a time and kept there until she calmed down, she was hit all over her body.

Betty's sister Bridie was beat more than most, she was more assertive and rebellious, the nuns had it in for Bridie for this reason, she was soon transferred to the Good Shepherd Convent Laundry where she received psychiatric treatment all her life, and died at the age of *fifty* she had a tragic life.

Betty was very upset when she witnessed her sister's abuse, she felt sorry for her and felt angry that she could do nothing to save her.

The atmosphere in the convent was very tense and gloomy she went from mass to work to bed, there was no personal freedom she pined for her family and home.

Betty's mother visited a few times a year and took the girls out for a few hours, but she felt angry at her mother because she was not able to go home for a visit during the time she had been incarcerated.

She was fearful that she may be sent to the Good Shepherd Covent like her sister.

The food was horrible and rationed, the girls received an egg at Christmas and she often went to bed hungry.

Her sister Bridie had a tooth removed by the dentist because she had toothache, and she had haemorrhaged during the night following the extraction.

One of the nuns plugged her gum until morning, Bridie felt very weak and for weeks after this incident, she was pale, tired it was suspected she was anaemic.

Mary also recalls she was infested with head lice for weeks on and off, she believed her head was worse in school, she was neglected in the convent.

She had started her periods at a young age, there was no preparation for puberty and totally inadequate sanitation.

She received no sex education and felt she was ignored, her emotional needs were entirely unmet. She felt like a work horse, and an object to be exploited at will.

When Betty was left in the convent she was underweight weighing under *six* stone, and had found it difficult to adjust to the outside world when she eventually left the convent.

Betty suffers with depression coupled with anxiety and panic attacks, she attributes this to her being institutionalised.

She is emotionally scarred from the past and doesn't like to talk about what happened back then.

Betty had not bonded with her mother and the family never reintegrated.

She never socialised and found it hard, it was a struggle, she kept a low profile when she lived in England often feeling lonely and lost.

She had low self esteem and no confidence, her sister taught her basic literacy and filled in all forms for her, jobs were hard going and she was wary of others.

Things for Betty have improved with the passage of time but still feels empty, sad and very often tearful.

PHOTOS OF TERESA & MARY

Teresa on the 6 & 9 O'Clock news headlines

Dublin remembers the Magdalene's 5 June 2018.
Teresa & Mary (Betty) In the garden of president Michael D. Higgins residence Phoenix Park, Dublin

Magdalene's Remembrance

Teresa with her friend her Husband Oliver and friend Mary (Betty)

Teresa with the presidents wife Mrs Higgins

Teresa & Mary with Colm O'Gorman who was first successful in his redress he is with Amnesty International and still works very hard for the survivors.

Irish Protestant Mother & Baby Homes

Once the news of Tuam hit the headlines, and since there has been a staggering amount of people coming forward from other institutions, news of the "Inmates" as some were called from the Catholic mother and baby homes broke internationally with vast response from other countries.

Unfortunately Protestant mother and baby homes have not had the same breaking news as the others, why? Is unclear.

It's said that more than *200* children of just one home in Dublin have been buried in unmarked graves.

Children born at Bethany home between *1922* and *1949* were also buried in unmarked graves, just like many others, but why, didn't alarm bells start ringing when all those deaths were happening?

Simply because people turned a blind eye, rather than face the wrath of the priest or minister they just kept Schtum.

Former residents of Bethany have told researchers that they were victims of neglect and physical abuse.

I read in a report that officials were told about appalling conditions for children but they did nothing, the headline read 'Starved to Death'

Records show that most of the children were days, weeks or months old when they died. Others showed clear evidence of neglect, one child reportedly died after crawling into a scalding hot pot of gruel. Many, who were adopted went to endure physical and sexual abuse.

Former Bethany survivor Derek Leinster has written a book called Hannah's Shame Available to buy on Amazon. Hannah's Shame is the inspirational story of one boy's Irish childhood spent in poverty because of the neglect at the Church of Ireland, of his lifelong search for who he is and his fight for justice.

Abandoned at birth by his mother in a children's home where illness, hunger and neglect were commonplace, fostered by an inordinately poor family and then living in poverty but ignored by the well-to-do community in which he was brought up, it is a story that will touch your heart, it is one of shame.

I had the privilege to speak briefly with Derek and promised him that this book would not only touch on a shameful Catholic church and the heartbreaking hurt they have caused thousands but that of the protestant and other religious orders too.

Another report I read in regard to the Protestant run homes told how a child who had been fostered out to a family had at the young age of around five or six had to do manual labour before having to walk several miles to school.

Why, I ask myself were there no follow up's on the children who had been fostered or adopted? Surely those responsible for the arrangements of the children being fostered and or adopted must for at least, for the child's first year visit those homes and conduct physical and written reports, those who were taken overseas for instance, there surely must have been an acting authority that undertook those duties?

This just goes to show how in the eyes of officials especially the church and the State that they were just a number and if there is monetary gain like with the church then they will just send you away in the hope that you become someone else's problem, out of sight, out of mind.

Ireland's shameful past, was not an isolated case those atrocities were happening all over the world, I have watched documentary's from Spain where this was going on, one in particular made me absolutely sick to the stomach to learn that in one hospital a dead child was kept in a fridge so that those who thought they lost their child and asked to see the child, would be handed a cold baby to further prove that their child had died.

I cannot get that image out of my head, and it does raise the question as to whether this may still be going on?

It doesn't matter if it was a mother and baby home, magdalene laundry, orphanage or other these horrific acts of mental, physical and or sexual abuse, it is wrong on so many levels and it went on, it may still going on? And it's now time that those criminals *(And that's what they are)* are held accountable and punished.

Only a sixteen mile drive from where I live now is Syllum Park Orphanage and yet another scandal *(Where does it stop?)* I have spoke to one elderly man whom I can't name for privacy reason and that we have still to continue to talk about his life in the orphanage, this man was distraught telling me the little he has already.

I'm talking about a man in his 70s who ended up in tears on the phone to me, for which I asked him to take a break and we would talk again.

I cannot explain how heartbreaking it was for me to listen to what he was telling me, I had to bite the side of my face to try and stop myself from crying, I mean, here I am listening to his story while trying to console him and telling him that he has nothing to be ashamed of, and I'm trying so hard for him not to realise I had tears streaming down my face.

A little now of a short story I read last year about another orphanage, this time I cannot name the orphanage or any other names related to this story for privacy reason.

But his shows how widespread all of the abuses are, and let me point out that i'm not in any way saying that all who run these institutions are committing these crimes, we must remember that there is good and bad in people and in many sectors, not necessarily all.

xxxx Story,

After being relinquished by his mother at the age of just *two*, xxxx was placed in several orphanages before arriving at the xxxx brothers orphanage in xxxx.

Brother xxxx came to the orphanage in *1953* and not long after his arrival he began to sexually abuse xx year old xxxx.

It has taken him *fifty-nine* years to get to the stage of being able talk about what happened.

xxxx said he was so ashamed when he got out he never told anyone that he went to that school, he said that he was sexually abused by brother xxxx three times a week for *two* years.

He said that he didn't talk to the other boys about it at the time, but was now aware that brother xxxx was abusing others as well, xxxx said he knew of *two* other boys who later committed suicide.

One day during a drive brother xxxx pulled the car over and began fondling xxxx who burst into tears, brother xxxx stopped, but some time later made xxxx come to his room, he made him undress and perform oral sex on him.

He felt he couldn't tell anyone for feeling ashamed and he felt there was none to tell, brother xxxx told xxxx that he was loving him like a father.

I'm shaking my head as I write this because while I and many others would be saying to ourselves what kind of father loves their child in this way? When really we know all to well that at that age a child knows no different if they haven't been taught that it is wrong.

He bought xxx a watch and cigarettes and gave him money, is it any wonder that at such a young age he thought this was right?

It seems to me that abuse is rife in religious organisations, as if it's not bad enough for those suffering outside religion, another story I read again last year didn't surprise me at all because I have heard similar stories before.

xxxx Story,

The first thing that xxxx noticed were, the white sheets hanging up in father xxxx room, forming a makeshift studio, it was in *1985* and as an *eleven* year old, she had previously mentioned her childhood aspirations to become a model in a very religious xxxx.

She told a commissioner of investigation that, the principle often pulled her out of class and send her to the presbytery to the touchy-feely priest.

He responded by offering to take some photos of her, when she walked in she saw the white sheets and lights set up, the priest had said to her, look at all this work I have done for you and she thought it would be okay because the principle had sent her there.

Despite feeling strange and uneasy, xxxx started posing for pictures, the priest had taken a few pictures, then, asked her to change into a white see-through shirt.

She said the shirt smelt like him and at first she refused, then he got angry and told her if she wanted to be a supermodel, then that was what he had to do, he also told her not to put any underwear on as the lines would be seen and ruin the photos.

xxxx said, the priest left the room for a while, while she put the shirt on, when he came back he asked her to pose like the model xxxx xxxxx he told her to stand this way and that way saying, he wanted to get her face at a certain angle, but she knew he was taking photos of her private parts.

He walked over to her and then proceeded to put his fingers inside her top, he was touching her breasts by then she was crying and shaking uncontrollably, she told him she wanted to go home to her grandmother.

As she was leaving the priest warned her that he was an important man in the town, she confided the abuse to a friend the next day.

They decided none would believe them so never told anyone, they thought they may be expelled from school, her mother had left when she was just three months old and her father was violent alcoholic, she was living with her grandmother who had Alzheimer's she felt if she told then she would be blamed so had nobody to confide in.

In the space of one hour her whole world had changed, she just saw the world in a completely different way after what he did to her.

So you see these are just a few examples of what I have already learned, there is so much more and a lot more that I, we are still unaware of because so many people have and still are suffering in silence.

Its people like you the reader, me the writer and all the many millions of others in the world who need to support those who fight for justice and to encourage those who are unable to speak of what they have and are going through to come forward and most importantly to understand that they are not sinner, they are not at fault.

POETRY

It was kindly agreed that I may include the following poems in this book, one which I had read via social media and the other, I was given to read whilst in Roscrea for the commemorations in *July 2019*.

Although some readers may find them a little disturbing they are a reflection of how many would have felt before, during and or after that dark time in history.

We must also take into account the feelings at that time of some if not all of the mothers, who by now you will understand felt nothing but shame followed by the emptiness with not being able to keep their child.

Many may have experienced an element of what is written in these poems, we also take into consideration that for some, these atrocities did take place and the world needs to know.

Many of the woman suffered in great silence having no voice some were told they must never speak of what happened to them and or others.

It's only through those who were able to tell their story that such crimes against humanity can be written in the said poems.

BEYOND THE WALL

Vulnerable, abandoned, godforsaken and neglected Impoverished, unfortunate and cruelly unprotected
The world outside oblivious, did no-one care at all?
Indifferent to the wretched stolen lives beyond the wall

Children raped and beaten and methodically brutalised
Sadistic violence commonplace but how come no-one realised?
Fatal beatings certified as accidental death
Impartial to they're suffering, no point in wasting breath

A child who was a "runner" could expect a Brother's fist
Battered with the Hurley stick, a broken leg or wrist
Dragged back to their torment, locked behind the iron gates
A never-ending nightmare, only dreaded hell awaits

The mentally defective, wanton women, "whores" and "prostitutes"
Pregnant out of wedlock, adolescent girls and destitute
Oppression, degradation and a system that was punitive
The selling of their babies, diabolically lucrative

Toiling in the laundries, they were little more than slaves
Worked to death then cruelly cast aside in unmarked graves
A daily dose of silence, prayer and gross humiliation
Spartan, cold, indefinite, their bleak incarceration

Alcohol and drug abuse, and mindless criminality
Help to numb the memory of terror and brutality
Misfits of society, they fight their private war
Shamefully betrayed absurdly locked away once more

Lies, deceit, conspiracies to cover up the truthWicked clerics free to rape and violate our youth
The Pope is in denial does he just not care at all?
Indifferent to those wretched stolen lives beyond the wall.

~ Carol Ellis, August 2018

THE ALTER OF MAMMAN

Just a teenager picking blackberries they were juicy, plump and black,
A terrible bang to the back of my head, I awoke lying on my back,
I realised I was almost naked my breasts all scratched and bruised,
Down there below I saw blood flow, I was raped and sexually abused.

I told no one my terrible secret, I will sometimes forget maybe?
Then it suddenly got much worse, I was pregnant with a little baby,
Mother was quick to spot the signs and figured my condition,
Getting rid of this dirty thing was their new and scared mission.

My father hit me across the face while spitting out whore and slut,
No neighbour is getting wind of this tomorrow we are getting shot,
He couldn't be listening to snide remarks about ovens and baking buns,
I was loaded at night in the PP's car and landed to the nuns.

Alone in a palace reception no public could ever tell,
I was owned by the devils children, I had entered the bowels of hell,
My cloths were taken from me, they changed my given name,
They cut to the very bony skull, my beautiful nut brown mane.

I was dressed in a faded grey uniform with hems below the knee,
My transformation was complete, I was no longer me,
Reverend mother read me the rules and slapped me across the face,
There was no provocation just to let me know my place.

A sleepless night on an iron bed I cried away the time,
Ten other girls slept in this fridge, to speak was a major crime,
I was started in the laundry and lost all sense of hope,
Water freezing, water boiling and the stench of basic soap.

I got beatings, slaps and punches, drove my spirit raging wild,
But I was outward, quite and docile to protect my unborn child,
Then when my labour started with that searing labour pain,
Lying on their hospital table no kindness could I gain.

That heartless sneering nazi nun then delivered her usual shout,
You enjoyed it going in you sinner, now suffer it coming out,
After a long torturous labour my baby son was born,
And he was worth it every pain, beating and every scorn.

Now once again I was somebody I was mammy to this lovely boy,
He grew strong and pink on his mother's milk, I never knew such joy,
At nursing time one Tuesday I rushed to feed my son,
His cot was empty, moved aside my precious boy was gone.

The nun said he had gone by car just at the break of day,
At this very moment he is in the air, bound for USA,
I split that searing bitches lip and knocked her to the floor,
My flight was well expected, there were three outside the door.

They tied my hands to a water pipe in the isolation wing,
They hit me with a fury, taking turns one by one,
You filthy whore from the filthy sewer how dare you strike a nun,
You will never raise your hand again when this punishment is done.

I had no way to protect myself from kick, punch and slap,
Then the reverend mother stopped them and produced her leather strap,
With the pain of her terrible scourging I was going round the bend,
Then mother got really savage and used the buckle end.

I saw that big buckle flash then exploded in my face,
I must have blacked out instantly as no mercy can I trace,
I awoke in the nurses station, I had lain there for three days,
My left eye was amputated they stitched my torn face.

A hideous scar ran down my face from my forehead to my chin,
My lips were sewn up crooked and formed an evil grin,
Some cotton wool and lint were my poor left eye had been,
I knew I was never leaving here, I could never again be seen.

The holy nun described my 'Accident' and how lucky I had been,
I slipped on the soapy laundry floor and struck the mangle machine,
How sweet and gentle their smile, how devout their downcast eyes,
They look like angelic creatures as they spin their dirty lies.

I am smuggling out this scribbled note in the evening laundry van,

He promised he would pass it on to someone in command,
When the nurse has gone off duty and it's all still in the night,
I will use this stolen scale blade to end my miserable life.

I'll control my time of dying, where I go I cannot tell,
Can anyone vouch for heaven? I can certainly vouch for hell.

~Lewis Keating July 2016

Mother & Baby Homes

A tribute to the mothers, the mothers who wore the shoes.

The mothers who wore the shoes stepped inside the doors,
Signed the ledger as the Mother made entrance within,
Preparing the sentence of the crime,
For breaking the sin forgiven by God,
Not forgiven here, in this cold place within,
Church and State created their own law,
A sentence so severe, cruelly placed on the mothers,
They wore the shoes, worked to the bone within,
By the mothers time to give birth to their babies here within,
No pain relief given, thats one of their laws,
Punished by the Holy cloth here within,
Mothers bringing babies into the world,
Not accepted by Church, State or Society at all,
Because the mother broke the original sin,
Left broken hearted, cot empty,
Baby taken by the hands of the holy cloth,
Mothers left empty, broken hearted,
Because they broke the sin,
The sin of the past,
Some day there will be justice for the atrocities within,
As the mothers wore the shoes within.

By Sheila O'Bryne

Another poem that sheila had written and would like added in the book. Which is a tribute to a baby angel Evelyn O'Gorman and mother Ann O'Gorman

Little angel baby Evelyn my search for you all these years,
My voice was drowned out, all these years, left lingering,
The important people didn't listen to your mother,
They shun me aside for my baby Evelyn to be recognised,
Groups that represented us,
They never considered both of us at all,
Your mother who became stronger,
And other mothers stood beside me to hear a beckoning call,
I know my baby Evelyn you are cherished with love,
I know you are in heavens garden,
Playing with the Besberaeh angels up above,
Someday your broken hearted mother,
Will reunite with you up in heaven above,
We can be together with happiness,
And cherished with our love,
Special survivor, mothers and loyal friends,
Stood together to recognise little angel Evelyn O'Gorman,
And mother Ann O'Gorman with our love.

By Sheila O'Bryne

CODE OF CANON LAW

Before and after I decided to read the Fifth Interim Report I thought it would be a good idea to take a look at the Canon Law according to the Catholic church.

The code of Canon law is very lengthy however, I picked out just a few that stood out and are relevant to the interim report.

Title I. Baptism
Can. 859

If because of distance, or other circumstances the one to be baptised cannot go or be brought to the parish church or to another church or oratory without grave inconvenience, baptism, CAN and MUST be conferred in another church or oratory, or even in another fitting place.

Can. 867

Parents are obliged to take care that infants are baptised in the first few weeks; as soon as possible after the birth, or even before it, they are to go to the pastor to request the sacrament for their child and to be prepared properly for it.

2. (An infant in danger of death is to be baptised WITHOUT DELAY.)

Can. 868

2. An infant of Catholic parents or even non-Catholic parents is baptised licitly in danger of death even against the will of the parents.

Title III. Funerals

Can. 1176

3. The church earnestly recommended that the pious custom of burying the bodies of the deceased be observed.

Can. 1181

Regarding offerings on the occasion of funeral rights, the prescripts of **Can. 1264** are to be observed, with caution, however, that there is to be no favouritism towards persons in the funeral and that the poor are not deprived of fitting funerals.

Can. 1182

When a burial has been completed, a record is to be made in the register of deaths according to the norm of particular law.

2.

The local ordinary CAN permit children whom the parents intended to baptise but who died before baptism to be given ecclesiastical funerals.

Can. 1184

Unless they gave some signs of repentance before death, the following must be deprived of ecclesiastical funerals. *(Bearing in mind here that infants and young children did NOT live long enough to repent)*

1. Notorious apostates, heretics and schismatics;

2. Those who choose cremation of their bodies for reasons contrary to Christian faith;

3. Other manifest sinners who cannot be granted ecclesiastic funerals without public scandal of the faithful. *(So, if a child/ teen, is raped or sexually abused, she is the one to be punished and branded a sinner.)*

FIFTH INTERIM REPORT

After reading the interim report I have picked some of which stands out adding my own thoughts and that of several of the survivors. *(Who wish to remain anonymous)*

INTRODUCTION.
2.
The terms of reference of the commission include, among other things, to investigate post-mortem practices and procedures in respect of children or mothers who died while resident in these institutions, including the reporting of deaths, burial arrangements and transfer of the remains to educational institutions for the purpose of anatomical examination.

3.
This report is concerned with the burial arrangements in the main institutions under investigation, and with transfer of remains to educational institutions for the purpose of anatomical examination. It is limited to burials and does not include any analysis of the causes of deaths or the registrations of deaths. These issues will be dealt with in the final report.

OTHER INSTITUTIONS BEING INVESTIGATED
4.
The other institutions being investigated by the commission are not covered in this report, for a variety of reasons.

Some of the other investigations do not have significant issues relating to burials either because they did not have any, or any significant number of deaths, or because the deaths did not occur in any institutions and the responsibility for burial did not lie with the institutions, for example; (Dunboyne, the castle).

There is very little information about deaths in some institutions, for example, (Kilrush) The commissions investigation of Regina Coeli is not yet sufficiently advanced. The deaths of all institutions will be analysed in the commissions final report and any further information on burials will also be included.

ILLEGITIMATE
6.

The term "illegitimate" Is not acceptable and should never had been applied to any child. However, the fact that it was used on any official documentation until 1988 when *'The status of children act 1987'* Came into effect.

The descriptions *Legitimate* and *illegitimate* are used in many of the documents used being analysed by the commission, In many cases, it is the description "illegitimate" which allows the commission to correctly identify the children covered by its terms of reference.

CONTEXT

9.

The commission is conscious that the report is not placed in the same social context of the times as the final report will be.

STILL BIRTHS

11.

It is well established that stillborn children and unbaptised children were not generally buried in consecrated grounds but in cillini. Sometimes the cillini was just outside the walls of the recognised ground. (Cillini may also have been used for people who were not considered to a Christian burial in a consecrated burial ground. For example, (people who died by suicide.) It is very likely that all children who were born in mother and baby homes were baptised. *(I ask then why were no children buried in consecrated grounds?)*

There were stillbirths in the institutions being investigated, stillbirths from Bethany were buried in Mount Jerome in Dublin but it is not clear where stillbirths were buried in other institutions? It seems unlikely that they were buried in the same grounds as baptised children. *(Contradiction here) I and I'm sure many others will agree that the nuns should be legally forced to answer all these questions.*

13.

It was not possible to register stillbirths until 1995 Maternity homes were obliged to report the number of stillbirths to the department of local Government and Public Health (Later the department of health) *Surely they would have some kind of record, because those children were born, they must have had at least the mothers name, and of which home they died?*

NUMBERS OF DEATHS

17.

The commission considers it important to try to trace all children who died and it has devoted considerable time and resources *(Which in my opinion should be paid by the Religious orders concerned)* To this particular exercise.

There are extensive records in some cases and very sparse in others. At this stage March 2019 the commission is close to finalising the detailed numbers and these will be included in the final report. *Due in March 2020*

19.

There are instances in Tuam children's home which are not in the register of deaths. The number of such discrepancies is very small and not yet resolved, In the commissions view there is very little basis for the theory that the children concerned did not die but were sold to America.

Children from Tuam were adopted to America, (As were children from nearly all institutions under investigation) These adoptions are generally recorded in the Tuam records it is not obvious why subterfuges would require to arrange such adoptions?

23.

There was no obligation on private burial grounds to keep a register of burials. However, these private burial grounds relevant to this report, Glasnevin, Mount Jerome and St Josephs Cemetery, Cork, did not keep proper records.

There is no evidence that any records of burials was kept in the Congregation of the Sacred Hearts of Jesus and Mary in respect of burials in Castlepollard and Sean Ross Abbey.

There was a canon law requirement, to keep records of burials. *(Hence why I looked over the Canon Law.)*

SUMMARY OF FINDINGS

1.

The major issue about burials arise in the cases of Bessborough and Tuam. It is not known where the vast majority of children who died are buried.

There is a small burial grounds of Bessborough which was opened in 1956 for members of the congregation. It seems to be assumed by the former residents and advocacy groups that this is also where the children who died at Bessborough are buried as there are occasional meetings and commemorations held there.

More than 900 children died at Bessborough yet, it has been established by the commission that only 64 children were buried there?

The congregation of the Sacred Hearts of Jesus and Mary who owned and ran Bessborough do not know where the other children are buried. *How could they not know?*

3.

The congregation of the Sacred Hearts of Jesus and Mary who owned these institutions provided the commission with an affidavit about burials generally and specifically about the Castlepollard and Sean Ross Abbey child burials but very little evidence was provided to support the statements in it.

The affidavit was, in many respects, speculative, inaccurate and misleading.

5.

The commission of investigation finds it very difficult to understand that no member of the congregation was able to say where the children who died in Bessborough are buried.

The entire fifth interim report can be read via www.gov.ie Like many others I find it extremely hard to understand why, by court of law the Catholic church are so untouchable?

So many mother's and siblings *(Survivors)* Have fought and waited for so many years to be given answers.

This is not an isolated situation, this is all over Ireland and beyond. There are many of these institutions darted all over the country run by the clergy who took it upon themselves to break their own rules, they took girls and young woman from their homes away from society because THEY said they had committed a sin by becoming pregnant out of wedlock.

I remember a long time ago speaking to a priest about why the church still have this outdated rule of no contraception? Considering and taking into account those who may have been raped or sexually abused, very often by people they know.

I asked him why would a man who abused his child walk free while that child is ostracised both within the church and society back then.

His only answer was *Penitence* If the man confesses to his sin made with sorrow and the intention of amendment he will be forgiven.

You could have knocked me down with a feather, the shock almost made me sick to my stomach.

I have spoken with several individuals in connection to the mother and baby homes who have told me stories of not only physical abuse but of sexual abuse within the homes and that of slavery.

The injustices that have been committed by the church yet no responsibility or apologies have been given to these woman or the children *(Now adults)* Who are not only looking for justice but to find their roots.

Stripped of your identity, made to work like a dog, have your child taken from your arms then eventually set free with no child to take home, for those who's children have died the majority don't even have a resting place to find peace.

No mother should have to endure this kind of brutality, not in the past, not now not ever.

Although, I have done some research, and viewed some footage, of the cruelty that those connected to the mother and baby homes had to endure, there is still so much more research to be done and sadly I have run out of time because this book had already been scheduled twice for publication.

That's not to say I won't do another book or rewrite this one in the future?

Again there would have been the final report on the findings of the commission of investigation, which, should have been published at the beginning of the year. But has now been postponed until *October 2020*.

Then the commemorations at SRA had been canceled due to the Coronavirus and travel restrictions until *May 2021*.

I am now being sent documentaries to watch and finding other investigative and news in regards interviews with some of the survivors, so there would have been so much more to write about had the book not been put on hold in *2019*.

However, I will include links where people can follow reports, read and view stories etc, I would love for you the reader to connect with the survivors, you do not have to have been connected to any of the institutions but it would be very much appreciated to know that many others are supporting the cause.

SO MANY QUESTIONS

And still no answers! Of course the story doesn't just lay with the illegal adoption of children, its much deeper than that.

In the photograph *(Page 53)* you see the entrance to the angels plot at SRA and there are many more like them, and so many survivors still waiting for answers.

There have also been so many meeting and talks not to mention excavations and still with no firm answers.

It seems that there is a lot of passing the buck and going round in circles, but who really has the answers? Why have they taken so long and why do they keep extending the date in which to reveal the finding of the excavations?

Time and time again they changed dates for the Interim Reports to be published and that's not just the latest report, as far as I'm led to believe they have done this with each report that has been done?

The laws in Ireland are of course different from that of the U.K and again of Scotland.

In Scotland we still very much live by the Roman Laws in some aspects, England is pretty much different again as are Ireland, as I said before we here in Scotland as adopted children can have full access to all our adopted records when we reach *eighteen* but not in Ireland.

People are frustrated, yet, while I understand there has to be a level of privacy in regard to adopted children especially if they were born in the mother and baby homes, I and others feel it is their basic human right to know exactly where they came from, what their real name was as I'm to believe that some still don't have that information.

In *2021* I will be filming a documentary which will involve four individuals and their stories.

I will also be setting up a group page that will invite many connected to not only the mother and baby homes, but the magdalene laundries and orphanages run by various religious orders.

This Facebook group will be open to all including and hoping that mothers who had children in those institutions can join they will have a place where they may feel comfortable in talking privately with specific people who will assure them of complete anonymity if they so wish.

There are many mothers still living who sadly have never discussed their time in the institutions nor told their families about a child they had given birth too, these woman are carrying a broken heart often to the grave, if they can have someone to talk to privately who will never discuss their situation to any other, it may give them some solace.

I have also been speaking with individuals from an orphanage who have inquired about telling their story, sadly again there has been incidences of abuses mentally, physically and sexually.

Those institutions who committed all those atrocities and inflicted such pain to others haven't got away with anything, because the hurt you cause others will always come back to haunt you.

ADDED NEWS

Irish Daily Star, Monday 27 July 2020

A total of *1,024* "illegitimate children" Died in SRA mother and baby home over a thirty-seven year period, with almost half of them *455*, officially listed as having died of a heart attack.

Shockingly, the official death figures published for the first time today also reveal, *128* children died from, Marasmus, meaning severe malnutrition.

Other disturbing causes of deaths include convulsions and exhaustion, while two babies died of sun and heat stroke.

Even more disturbingly, one child died from acute heart failure, due to chocking on porridge.

The children who died ranged in age from just, one minute old, to seventeen years old, the teenager dying in St Gerard's hospital.

The number of children who died at SRA is higher than the registered deaths in the Tuam mother and baby home where *796* children died, as well as *817* in Bessborough in Cork.

SRA was run by the Sacred Hearts of Jesus and Mary, in Roscrea, Tipperary from *1932* to around *1970*, the same order of nuns who ran castle Pollarding Co Westmeath as well as Bessborough Institutions in Cork.

Catherine Corless who uncovered the names of the children in team home between *1925* and *1961* said; this is horrifying.

Those poor children, you wonder? Were they just putting down anything for the causes of death or did the children actually die this way?

Twenty-nine mothers died, and the majority of the deaths were related to pregnancy or childbirth.

Michael Donovan a Sinn Fein Councillor, worked as a gardener in SRA in the *1980s* he has given a statement to the commission of inquiry stating that he saw tiny bones the area now known as the Angels Plot.

Michael has stated that he is sick to the stomach at this news, he like many others are sick, tearful and shocked especially now they know that more than expected children died there, although deep down they knew this anyway, but to have it confirmed must be a terrible shock to the system.

Teresa Collins; 'Tell the truth…It will come out'

Teresa born in SRA in *1963* has revealed her father, whom she found in *2017* has tragically passed away, both Teresa and her dad Billy were overjoyed to meet in *2017* after years of searching.

They formed a loving bond until his death last January, Teresa has come out in support of the rights to identity, saying; *Adoptees have the right to their background "No matter the circumstances".*

She told the paper, while I understand that some fathers and mothers don't want to be involved in their Childs life, the child wants to know who they are…

It doesn't matter what the circumstances are, it's our identity, I would say to mothers, tell your children the truth or it will come back to bite you.

We grow up, we find out and it's important to know we will find out.

Teresa's mother didn't tell her who her father was, she requested her files and asked for information on her father, her father's name was down on the files, something that never happens, she was lucky.

Cont...

As reported by Peter Glesson in The Nenagh Guardian dated August *8, 2020*

Over *1,000* Babies Died in Home

Campaigners urge publication of report on Sean Ross Abbey mother and baby home.

A local woman who spent the first three months of her life in the Sean Ross Abbey mother and baby home in Roscrea has said she feels lucky to be alive as it emerged that over *1,000* babies died in the institution over a *thirty-seven*—year period.

Ms Collins, who's unmarried mother gave birth to her in *1963* in the home, is a member of a Facebook group of survivors who have obtained death certificates for *1,024* infants and children.

The group has also established from a trawl of deaths certificates that *twenty-nine* mothers dies in the home during the period, the majority relating to pregnancy or childbirth.

Ms Collins also said; *She and other members of the Facebook group are now eager, to establish if remains of the people who died in the home are still lying in unmarked graves? On the site, the mother and baby home commission set up to investigate practices and deaths in Sean Ross Abbey and other mother and baby homes in the State?*

A geographical survey was carried out *twenty* months ago, but Ms Collins said she and other members of the group would like to see further digs to look for remains on the site.

Ms Collins said: *She wanted to see the report published as soon as possible as victims deserve answers.*

RESOURCES

The delay in publishing a final report and the fact that redress for victims of the homes will not be considered until the final report has been published has been criticised by survivors, including the Coalition of Mother and Baby Home Survivors (CMABS). Paul Redmond, chairperson of CMABS, said that many survivors are now elderly and have already died since the revelations about Tuam first emerged, and that, This is yet another delaying tactic by the Government to deny survivors truth and justice. The current inquiry is already too limited and excludes many survivors and this delay will now ensure that thousands more survivors are denied justice by death.

Additional Information/Resources

https://en.wikipedia.org/wiki/Irish_Examiner

https://en.wikipedia.org/wiki/Health_Service_Executive_(Ireland)

https://en.wikipedia.org/wiki/Tusla

https://en.wikipedia.org/wiki/Bon_Secours_Mother_and_Baby_Home

https://www.nenaghguardian.ie

5th Interim Report

https://assets.gov.ie/26901/6de0eb1f8c4647b-da67985e2a4428e37.pdf

What to watch

Al Jazeers Mother & Baby Documentary Pt 1
https://youtu.be/F65Mc3oBylk
Al Jazeers Mother & Baby Documentary Pt 2
https://youtu.be/Zq_aXARjEs

Coming soon!

SOFA TALK MEDIA

My social media links, follow me to hear my podcasts and updates on my forthcoming documentary April 2021.

https://twitter.com/sofatalkmedia
https://www.facebook.com/sofatalkmedia/
Website: belindaconnissofficial.org
www.insideoutlastyle.com

If you are connected to any of the mother and baby homes, magdalene laundries or orphanages and would like to tell your story, and or be part of forthcoming documentary's then feel free to get in touch via the contact form on my website.

DEDICATION

'Behind Closed Doors' Written in dedication to the survivors of the mother and baby home era.

For their biological parents, some of whom have been found and those still to be found, and for those who have had to keep their secret buried deep within their hearts who feel/felt unable to tell their story, including those who had sadly to take their secret to their grave.

Lastly, for all the mothers & children who were sadly taken too soon, many of whom *(At the time of writing)* Have had no dignified burial nor gravestone that includes their identity.

May they forever rest in eternal peace in the arms of God

A NOTE FROM THE AUTHOR

Those who follow me on social media will already know that my aim in writing Behind Closed Doors is to help raise funds, for the committee who work tirelessly in order to carry on with the incredible work they do every year in bringing those together who are connected to the mother and baby homes.

Although it has been a long process with several obstacles along the way, I have done the best I can in terms of research, including talking with several people about their experiences.

I have also included in the book not only photos I've taken, Unless otherwise stated, but also stories and poems from various people who have given me permission to do so.

There are statements and or newspaper articles in the book that some people may have already known about, the purpose of including them here and credits given to the related article where necessary, is for those who don't know nor understand what went on in the subject matter.

I am not personally connected, or not that I know of yet, to any of the mother and baby homes other than supporting them in their fight for justice.

Although who knows? My family origins are from both sides of Ireland, and I may very well have family members who were incarcerated in such institutions?

The book has proven to be a little of a challenge, mostly due to unforeseen circumstances that set me back just over a years work. The original date of the book should have been published in *March/April 2019*, but two weeks prior to Christmas *2018* my husband was diagnosed with cancer.

The last thing on my mind was writing, so the date was then pushed back to *July 2020* so that I could include a write-up on a Docucast *(A short Documentary)* that was meant to be filmed in *April 2020*.

This would coincide with the *July 2020* commemoration, yet again, it had been pushed-back due to being on lockdown from Coronavirus. At times my heart wasn't in it, there were so many times when I just didn't have the energy mentally or physically.

Some days I had to push myself, I could have a good run one day and write lots then nothing for weeks at a time.

It is also the first time I have taken to formatting and editing myself, mainly because as you will know it cost a pretty penny to have a copy editor do it for me, and as I'm trying to raise funds I preferred to do it myself. As promised, I will be donating a percentage of the first year of sales to SRA Committee, which would have been donated on the *July 2021* commemorations, however, the date has now changed to *May 2021* all being well with government guidelines and assuming it is safe to travel.

If the committee prefer to wait until the July which will give them a full year's percentage then thats what will happen.

I will also upload to my website and social media a live feed of the donation being handed to the committee.

So please be kind, if I have made any mistakes in my editing *(Fingers crossed, that is not the case)* Just remember the book has been written for a cause close to not only my heart but that of the survivors.

VARIOUS PHOTOS

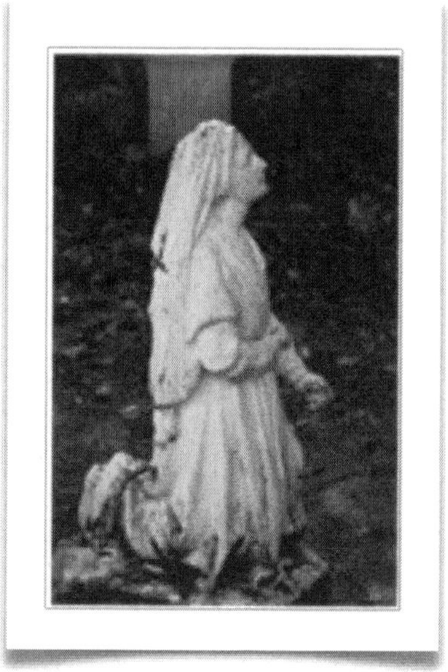

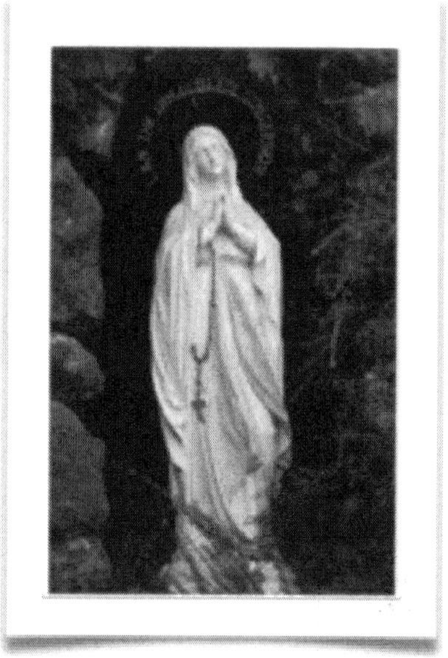

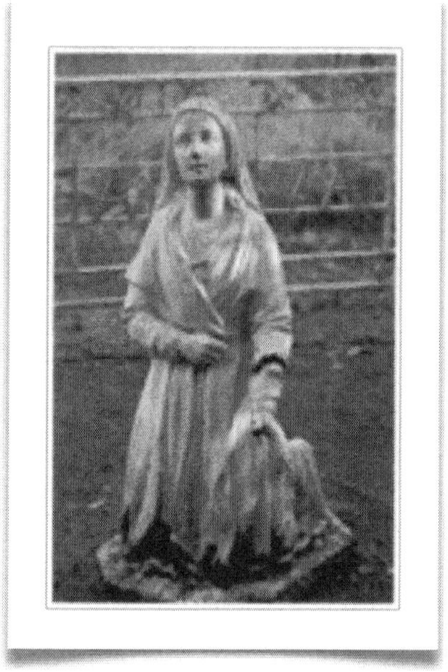

Statue in memory of Anthony Lee *(Michael Anthony Hess)* Arranged by Michael Donovan

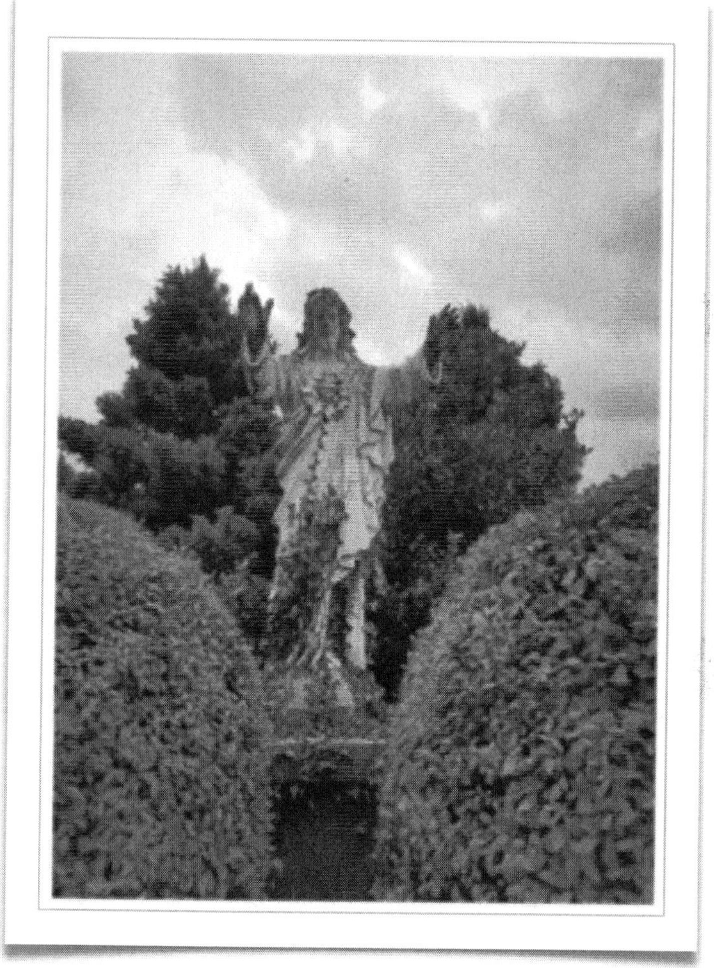

ABOUT THE AUTHOR

Belinda Conniss is an author/novelist who has published two non-fiction books, one fictional short story and a book of poetry.

She is a Freelance writer/editor and an advocate, she enjoys theatre and writing articles on various subjects.

A keen amateur photographer and has most recently been working on plans for future Podcasts/Documentary's

***

Twitter: @BelindaConniss7
Facebook @belindaconnisspublishedauthor | @sofatalkmedia

WWW.INSIDEOUTLASTYLE.COM

Printed in Great Britain
by Amazon